**TEACHER'S PET PUBLICATIONS**

PUZZLE PACK
for
The Slave Dancer

based on the book by
Paula Fox

Written by
William T. Collins

© 2005 Teacher's Pet Publications
All Rights Reserved

The materials in this packet are copyrighted
by Teacher's Pet Publications, Inc.

These pages may be duplicated by the purchaser
for use in the purchaser's own classroom.

Copying any of these materials and distributing them
for any other purpose is a violation of the copyright laws.

© 2005 Teacher's Pet Publications, Inc.
www.tpet.com

INTRODUCTION
If you already own the LitPlan for this title, this Puzzle Pack will refresh your Unit Resource Materials and Vocabulary Resource Materials sections plus give you additional materials you can substitute into the tests. If you do not already have a complete LitPlan, these pages will give you some supplemental materials to use with your own plan. There are two main groups of materials: one set for unit words (such as characters' names, symbols, places, etc.) and one set for vocabulary words associated with the book.

WORD LIST
There is a word list for both the unit words and the vocabulary words. These lists show you which words are being used in the materials and the clues or definitions being used for those words. You may want to give students a word list with clues/definitions to help them, or you may want students to only have a word list (without clues/definitions) if you want them to work a little harder. Both are available for duplication. The word lists can also be your "calling key" for the bingo games.

FILL IN THE BLANK AND MATCHING
There are 4 each of the fill in the blank and matching worksheets for both the unit and vocabulary words. These pages can be used either as extra worksheets for students or as objective parts of a unit test. They can be done individually if students need extra help or as a whole class activity to review the material covered.

MAGIC SQUARES
The magic squares not only reinforce the material covered but also work on reasoning and math skills. Many teachers have told us that their students really enjoy doing these!

WORD SEARCH PUZZLES
The word search words go in all directions, as indicated on your answer keys. Two of the word search puzzles have the clues listed rather than the words. This makes the puzzle a little more difficult, but it reinforces the material better. Two word search puzzles have words only for students who find the clue puzzles too difficult.

CROSSWORD PUZZLES
Both unit and vocabulary word sections have 4 crossword puzzles.

BINGO CARDS
There are 32 individual bingo cards for the unit words and 32 individual bingo cards for the vocabulary words. You can use your word list as a "call list," calling the words at random and marking them off of your list as you go, or you could use the flash cards by cutting them apart and drawing the words at random from a hat (or box or whatever). To make a better review, you might ask for the definition and spelling of each word as you call it out–or you could call out the definitions and have students tell you the words they need to look for on the puzzle.

JUGGLE LETTERS
The vocabulary juggle letter game is intended to help students learn the spellings of the words. One sheet has the definitions listed on it as an extra help for students who need it or to reinforce the definitions if you choose to do so.

FLASH CARDS
We've included a set of vocabulary flash cards you can duplicate, cut, and fold for your students. Some teachers make a few sets for general use by the class; others make a set for each student. Some teachers duplicate them for each student and have the students cut & fold their own. You can cut out just the words and put them in a hat, have each student pick out one word and write the definition and a sentence for that word. Students then swap words and papers, with the next student adding a sentence of his own under the last one. You can have students swap as many times as you like. Each time the student will read the sentences written prior to his own and then add a sentence. You can cut out the words and definitions separately and play "I Have; Who Has?" Each student in the room draws a word and definition. The first student says, "I have (the name of the word). Who has the definition?" The student with the definition reads it then says, "I have (the name of the vocabulary word she has). Who has the definition?" The round continues until all words and definitions have been given.

Slave Dancer Word List

No.	Word	Clue/Definition
1.	AFRICA	Where The Moonlight will pick up slaves
2.	AGATHA	Jessie's dead father's cranky sister: Aunt ___
3.	APPRENTICE	Jessie did this under apothecary
4.	BEAULIEU	Jessie's father's French surname
5.	BEN	Took Spark's place: ___ Stout
6.	BENIN	African bay: Bight of ___
7.	BETTY	Jessie's sister
8.	BLOCKADE	Englishmen trying to stop slave trade: British ___
9.	BOLLWEEVIL	Captain's nickname for Jessie
10.	BOOM	Ras and Jessie hung onto it in the water
11.	CANDLES	Needed by Jessie's mother to sew at night
12.	CARRE	New Orleans' French Quarter: Vieux ___
13.	CASKS	Wooden kegs kept in the hold that held water
14.	CAWTHORNE	Ship's captain
15.	CHARLESTON	Final destination of ship
16.	CHICKEN	First sign of life on deserted land
17.	COCKROACH	Oddly comforting sight upon Jessie's waking
18.	CONGO	New Orleans spot for slave festivity: ___ Square
19.	CRADLE	String game Purvis played with Jessie: Cat's ___
20.	CREOLE	Louisianian of French ancestry
21.	CUBA	Place where slaves will be sold
22.	CURRY	Ship's cook
23.	DANIEL	Old Mississippi escaped black man who helps boys
24.	FIFE	Jessie's instrument
25.	FLYING	Carved on Jessie's mother's sewing box: ___ fish
26.	GALLEY	Where Curry prepared lentil soup
27.	GOLD	Slave trade: Black ___
28.	HAMMOCK	Jessie's bed on ship
29.	HOPE	Pushed Jessie on while dogpaddling
30.	IBOS	Captain won't take any of them
31.	JESSIE	Kidnapped New Orleans boy
32.	LIME	Used to try to clear stench from hold: chloride of ___
33.	LOUT	Aunt Agatha's name for Jessie: Bayou ___
34.	MACAROON	Defective black
35.	MOONLIGHT	Slaving ship: The ___
36.	NED	Ship's carpenter: ___ Grime
37.	NEEDLE	Object used to support Bollier family
38.	PRESSED	Pressganged or forced into ship's service
39.	PRIVATEERS	Individuals profiting on slave trade
40.	PURVIS	Kidnapper Jessie came to trust
41.	RAFT	Craft on which Claudius and Purvis dumped Jessie
42.	RAS	Black boy who survives with Jessie
43.	REVENUE	Patrols U.S. shores: U.S. ___ Cutters
44.	SHARKS	Crescent-mouthed maggots with stitched teeth
45.	SHROUDS	Ropes that support the mast
46.	SLAVE	Corner of St. Louis and Chartres Streets: ___ Market
47.	SPARK	Cawthorne's first mate
48.	STAR	Slave woman Jessie saw in the Vieux Carre
49.	SWIM	Plea that served Jessie in the end: Oh ___!
50.	THIRTEEN	Slave dancer's age

Slave Dancer Fill In The Blank 1

1. New Orleans spot for slave festivity: ___ Square
2. Captain won't take any of them
3. Final destination of ship
4. Corner of St. Louis and Chartres Streets: ___ Market
5. Craft on which Claudius and Purvis dumped Jessie
6. New Orleans' French Quarter: Vieux ____
7. Cawthorne's first mate
8. Ship's captain
9. Jessie's father's French surname
10. Old Mississippi escaped black man who helps boys
11. Individuals profiting on slave trade
12. Took Spark's place: ___ Stout
13. Jessie did this under apothecary
14. Jessie's dead father's cranky sister: Aunt ___
15. Jessie's sister
16. Needed by Jessie's mother to sew at night
17. Slave trade: Black ___
18. Jessie's bed on ship
19. Pressganged or forced into ship's service
20. Pushed Jessie on while dogpaddling

Slave Dancer Fill In The Blank 1 Answer Key

CONGO	1. New Orleans spot for slave festivity: ___ Square
IBOS	2. Captain won't take any of them
CHARLESTON	3. Final destination of ship
SLAVE	4. Corner of St. Louis and Chartres Streets: ___ Market
RAFT	5. Craft on which Claudius and Purvis dumped Jessie
CARRE	6. New Orleans' French Quarter: Vieux ___
SPARK	7. Cawthorne's first mate
CAWTHORNE	8. Ship's captain
BEAULIEU	9. Jessie's father's French surname
DANIEL	10. Old Mississippi escaped black man who helps boys
PRIVATEERS	11. Individuals profiting on slave trade
BEN	12. Took Spark's place: ___ Stout
APPRENTICE	13. Jessie did this under apothecary
AGATHA	14. Jessie's dead father's cranky sister: Aunt ___
BETTY	15. Jessie's sister
CANDLES	16. Needed by Jessie's mother to sew at night
GOLD	17. Slave trade: Black ___
HAMMOCK	18. Jessie's bed on ship
PRESSED	19. Pressganged or forced into ship's service
HOPE	20. Pushed Jessie on while dogpaddling

Slave Dancer Fill In The Blank 2

_____

_____

_____

_____

_____

_____

_____

_____

_____

_____

_____

_____

_____

_____

_____

_____

_____

_____

_____

_____

1. Plea that served Jessie in the end: Oh ____!

2. New Orleans' French Quarter: Vieux ____

3. Slave woman Jessie saw in the Vieux Carre

4. Captain's nickname for Jessie

5. Where Curry prepared lentil soup

6. African bay: Bight of ___

7. Oddly comforting sight upon Jessie's waking

8. Slave dancer's age

9. Slave trade: Black ___

10. Object used to support Bollier family

11. String game Purvis played with Jessie: Cat's ___

12. Needed by Jessie's mother to sew at night

13. Individuals profiting on slave trade

14. Crescent-mouthed maggots with stitched teeth

15. Jessie's father's French surname

16. Place where slaves will be sold

17. Used to try to clear stench from hold: chloride of ____

18. Cawthorne's first mate

19. Carved on Jessie's mother's sewing box: ___ fish

20. Black boy who survives with Jessie

Slave Dancer Fill In The Blank 2 Answer Key

SWIM	1. Plea that served Jessie in the end: Oh ____!
CARRE	2. New Orleans' French Quarter: Vieux ____
STAR	3. Slave woman Jessie saw in the Vieux Carre
BOLLWEEVIL	4. Captain's nickname for Jessie
GALLEY	5. Where Curry prepared lentil soup
BENIN	6. African bay: Bight of ___
COCKROACH	7. Oddly comforting sight upon Jessie's waking
THIRTEEN	8. Slave dancer's age
GOLD	9. Slave trade: Black ___
NEEDLE	10. Object used to support Bollier family
CRADLE	11. String game Purvis played with Jessie: Cat's ___
CANDLES	12. Needed by Jessie's mother to sew at night
PRIVATEERS	13. Individuals profiting on slave trade
SHARKS	14. Crescent-mouthed maggots with stitched teeth
BEAULIEU	15. Jessie's father's French surname
CUBA	16. Place where slaves will be sold
LIME	17. Used to try to clear stench from hold: chloride of ____
SPARK	18. Cawthorne's first mate
FLYING	19. Carved on Jessie's mother's sewing box: ___ fish
RAS	20. Black boy who survives with Jessie

Slave Dancer Fill In The Blank 3

_____
_____
_____
_____
_____
_____
_____
_____
_____
_____
_____
_____
_____
_____
_____
_____
_____
_____
_____
_____

1. Object used to support Bollier family
2. Place where slaves will be sold
3. Slave trade: Black ___
4. Englishmen trying to stop slave trade: British ____
5. Jessie's dead father's cranky sister: Aunt ___
6. Ras and Jessie hung onto it in the water
7. Louisianian of French ancestry
8. Pushed Jessie on while dogpaddling
9. String game Purvis played with Jessie: Cat's ___
10. Final destination of ship
11. Jessie's sister
12. Where The Moonlight will pick up slaves
13. Wooden kegs kept in the hold that held water
14. Aunt Agatha's name for Jessie: Bayou ___
15. Needed by Jessie's mother to sew at night
16. Kidnapper Jessie came to trust
17. Kidnapped New Orleans boy
18. Plea that served Jessie in the end: Oh ____!
19. Jessie did this under apothecary
20. Took Spark's place: ___ Stout

Slave Dancer Fill In The Blank 3 Answer Key

NEEDLE	1. Object used to support Bollier family
CUBA	2. Place where slaves will be sold
GOLD	3. Slave trade: Black ___
BLOCKADE	4. Englishmen trying to stop slave trade: British ___
AGATHA	5. Jessie's dead father's cranky sister: Aunt ___
BOOM	6. Ras and Jessie hung onto it in the water
CREOLE	7. Louisianian of French ancestry
HOPE	8. Pushed Jessie on while dogpaddling
CRADLE	9. String game Purvis played with Jessie: Cat's ___
CHARLESTON	10. Final destination of ship
BETTY	11. Jessie's sister
AFRICA	12. Where The Moonlight will pick up slaves
CASKS	13. Wooden kegs kept in the hold that held water
LOUT	14. Aunt Agatha's name for Jessie: Bayou ___
CANDLES	15. Needed by Jessie's mother to sew at night
PURVIS	16. Kidnapper Jessie came to trust
JESSIE	17. Kidnapped New Orleans boy
SWIM	18. Plea that served Jessie in the end: Oh ___!
APPRENTICE	19. Jessie did this under apothecary
BEN	20. Took Spark's place: ___ Stout

Slave Dancer Fill In The Blank 4

_____

_____

_____

_____

_____

_____

_____

_____

_____

_____

_____

_____

_____

_____

_____

_____

_____

_____

_____

_____

1. Aunt Agatha's name for Jessie: Bayou ___
2. Object used to support Bollier family
3. Wooden kegs kept in the hold that held water
4. Black boy who survives with Jessie
5. Ship's cook
6. Crescent-mouthed maggots with stitched teeth
7. Jessie's dead father's cranky sister: Aunt ___
8. First sign of life on deserted land
9. Final destination of ship
10. Kidnapped New Orleans boy
11. Kidnapper Jessie came to trust
12. Jessie's father's French surname
13. String game Purvis played with Jessie: Cat's ___
14. Patrols U.S. shores: U.S. ___ Cutters
15. Jessie's sister
16. Jessie's instrument
17. Used to try to clear stench from hold: chloride of ___
18. Craft on which Claudius and Purvis dumped Jessie
19. Slave dancer's age
20. Where The Moonlight will pick up slaves

Slave Dancer Fill In The Blank 4 Answer Key

LOUT	1. Aunt Agatha's name for Jessie: Bayou ___
NEEDLE	2. Object used to support Bollier family
CASKS	3. Wooden kegs kept in the hold that held water
RAS	4. Black boy who survives with Jessie
CURRY	5. Ship's cook
SHARKS	6. Crescent-mouthed maggots with stitched teeth
AGATHA	7. Jessie's dead father's cranky sister: Aunt ___
CHICKEN	8. First sign of life on deserted land
CHARLESTON	9. Final destination of ship
JESSIE	10. Kidnapped New Orleans boy
PURVIS	11. Kidnapper Jessie came to trust
BEAULIEU	12. Jessie's father's French surname
CRADLE	13. String game Purvis played with Jessie: Cat's ___
REVENUE	14. Patrols U.S. shores: U.S. ___ Cutters
BETTY	15. Jessie's sister
FIFE	16. Jessie's instrument
LIME	17. Used to try to clear stench from hold: chloride of ___
RAFT	18. Craft on which Claudius and Purvis dumped Jessie
THIRTEEN	19. Slave dancer's age
AFRICA	20. Where The Moonlight will pick up slaves

Slave Dancer Matching 1

___ 1. CRADLE
___ 2. GOLD
___ 3. BLOCKADE
___ 4. BETTY
___ 5. CAWTHORNE
___ 6. CREOLE
___ 7. RAS
___ 8. CURRY
___ 9. IBOS
___ 10. RAFT
___ 11. MOONLIGHT
___ 12. SPARK
___ 13. APPRENTICE
___ 14. BOLLWEEVIL
___ 15. HOPE
___ 16. SLAVE
___ 17. SWIM
___ 18. DANIEL
___ 19. STAR
___ 20. CASKS
___ 21. CHARLESTON
___ 22. SHROUDS
___ 23. CANDLES
___ 24. NEEDLE
___ 25. AGATHA

A. Black boy who survives with Jessie
B. Jessie's dead father's cranky sister: Aunt ___
C. Corner of St. Louis and Chartres Streets: ___ Market
D. Ship's cook
E. Needed by Jessie's mother to sew at night
F. Final destination of ship
G. Pushed Jessie on while dogpaddling
H. Craft on which Claudius and Purvis dumped Jessie
I. Ship's captain
J. Object used to support Bollier family
K. Slave woman Jessie saw in the Vieux Carre
L. Captain won't take any of them
M. Slave trade: Black ___
N. Ropes that support the mast
O. Old Mississippi escaped black man who helps boys
P. String game Purvis played with Jessie: Cat's ___
Q. Cawthorne's first mate
R. Louisianian of French ancestry
S. Jessie's sister
T. Wooden kegs kept in the hold that held water
U. Slaving ship: The ___
V. Plea that served Jessie in the end: Oh ___!
W. Jessie did this under apothecary
X. Englishmen trying to stop slave trade: British ___
Y. Captain's nickname for Jessie

Slave Dancer Matching 1 Answer Key

P - 1. CRADLE	A.	Black boy who survives with Jessie
M - 2. GOLD	B.	Jessie's dead father's cranky sister: Aunt ___
X - 3. BLOCKADE	C.	Corner of St. Louis and Chartres Streets: ___ Market
S - 4. BETTY	D.	Ship's cook
I - 5. CAWTHORNE	E.	Needed by Jessie's mother to sew at night
R - 6. CREOLE	F.	Final destination of ship
A - 7. RAS	G.	Pushed Jessie on while dogpaddling
D - 8. CURRY	H.	Craft on which Claudius and Purvis dumped Jessie
L - 9. IBOS	I.	Ship's captain
H - 10. RAFT	J.	Object used to support Bollier family
U - 11. MOONLIGHT	K.	Slave woman Jessie saw in the Vieux Carre
Q - 12. SPARK	L.	Captain won't take any of them
W - 13. APPRENTICE	M.	Slave trade: Black ___
Y - 14. BOLLWEEVIL	N.	Ropes that support the mast
G - 15. HOPE	O.	Old Mississippi escaped black man who helps boys
C - 16. SLAVE	P.	String game Purvis played with Jessie: Cat's ___
V - 17. SWIM	Q.	Cawthorne's first mate
O - 18. DANIEL	R.	Louisianian of French ancestry
K - 19. STAR	S.	Jessie's sister
T - 20. CASKS	T.	Wooden kegs kept in the hold that held water
F - 21. CHARLESTON	U.	Slaving ship: The ___
N - 22. SHROUDS	V.	Plea that served Jessie in the end: Oh ____!
E - 23. CANDLES	W.	Jessie did this under apothecary
J - 24. NEEDLE	X.	Englishmen trying to stop slave trade: British ____
B - 25. AGATHA	Y.	Captain's nickname for Jessie

Slave Dancer Matching 2

___ 1. NED
___ 2. MACAROON
___ 3. CARRE
___ 4. CURRY
___ 5. NEEDLE
___ 6. PRIVATEERS
___ 7. GALLEY
___ 8. IBOS
___ 9. DANIEL
___ 10. STAR
___ 11. BENIN
___ 12. SWIM
___ 13. THIRTEEN
___ 14. CASKS
___ 15. LOUT
___ 16. BLOCKADE
___ 17. CONGO
___ 18. RAFT
___ 19. AFRICA
___ 20. AGATHA
___ 21. BOOM
___ 22. BEN
___ 23. SLAVE
___ 24. BOLLWEEVIL
___ 25. CREOLE

A. Louisianian of French ancestry
B. Where The Moonlight will pick up slaves
C. Englishmen trying to stop slave trade: British ____
D. African bay: Bight of ___
E. Wooden kegs kept in the hold that held water
F. Slave dancer's age
G. Captain's nickname for Jessie
H. Jessie's dead father's cranky sister: Aunt ___
I. Ship's cook
J. Craft on which Claudius and Purvis dumped Jessie
K. Old Mississippi escaped black man who helps boys
L. Where Curry prepared lentil soup
M. Object used to support Bollier family
N. Individuals profiting on slave trade
O. Slave woman Jessie saw in the Vieux Carre
P. New Orleans spot for slave festivity: ___ Square
Q. Captain won't take any of them
R. Plea that served Jessie in the end: Oh ____!
S. Corner of St. Louis and Chartres Streets: ___ Market
T. Defective black
U. Ras and Jessie hung onto it in the water
V. New Orleans' French Quarter: Vieux ____
W. Ship's carpenter: ___ Grime
X. Aunt Agatha's name for Jessie: Bayou ___
Y. Took Spark's place: ___ Stout

Slave Dancer Matching 2 Answer Key

W - 1. NED		A. Louisianian of French ancestry
T - 2. MACAROON		B. Where The Moonlight will pick up slaves
V - 3. CARRE		C. Englishmen trying to stop slave trade: British ___
I - 4. CURRY		D. African bay: Bight of ___
M - 5. NEEDLE		E. Wooden kegs kept in the hold that held water
N - 6. PRIVATEERS		F. Slave dancer's age
L - 7. GALLEY		G. Captain's nickname for Jessie
Q - 8. IBOS		H. Jessie's dead father's cranky sister: Aunt ___
K - 9. DANIEL		I. Ship's cook
O -10. STAR		J. Craft on which Claudius and Purvis dumped Jessie
D -11. BENIN		K. Old Mississippi escaped black man who helps boys
R -12. SWIM		L. Where Curry prepared lentil soup
F -13. THIRTEEN		M. Object used to support Bollier family
E -14. CASKS		N. Individuals profiting on slave trade
X -15. LOUT		O. Slave woman Jessie saw in the Vieux Carre
C -16. BLOCKADE		P. New Orleans spot for slave festivity: ___ Square
P -17. CONGO		Q. Captain won't take any of them
J -18. RAFT		R. Plea that served Jessie in the end: Oh ___!
B -19. AFRICA		S. Corner of St. Louis and Chartres Streets: ___ Market
H -20. AGATHA		T. Defective black
U -21. BOOM		U. Ras and Jessie hung onto it in the water
Y -22. BEN		V. New Orleans' French Quarter: Vieux ___
S -23. SLAVE		W. Ship's carpenter: ___ Grime
G -24. BOLLWEEVIL		X. Aunt Agatha's name for Jessie: Bayou ___
A -25. CREOLE		Y. Took Spark's place: ___ Stout

Slave Dancer Matching 3

___ 1. GALLEY   A. Where Curry prepared lentil soup
___ 2. AFRICA   B. Used to try to clear stench from hold: chloride of ____
___ 3. GOLD   C. Corner of St. Louis and Chartres Streets: ___ Market
___ 4. JESSIE   D. Louisianian of French ancestry
___ 5. CREOLE   E. Carved on Jessie's mother's sewing box: ___ fish
___ 6. SHROUDS   F. Plea that served Jessie in the end: Oh ____!
___ 7. LIME   G. Cawthorne's first mate
___ 8. SPARK   H. Final destination of ship
___ 9. CHARLESTON   I. Jessie's father's French surname
___10. BEN   J. Ropes that support the mast
___11. BENIN   K. Captain's nickname for Jessie
___12. CANDLES   L. Defective black
___13. FLYING   M. Crescent-mouthed maggots with stitched teeth
___14. IBOS   N. African bay: Bight of ___
___15. BETTY   O. Black boy who survives with Jessie
___16. MACAROON   P. Slave woman Jessie saw in the Vieux Carre
___17. SWIM   Q. Where The Moonlight will pick up slaves
___18. AGATHA   R. Needed by Jessie's mother to sew at night
___19. SLAVE   S. Jessie's sister
___20. BEAULIEU   T. Slave trade: Black ___
___21. STAR   U. Captain won't take any of them
___22. CAWTHORNE   V. Took Spark's place: ___ Stout
___23. SHARKS   W. Ship's captain
___24. RAS   X. Kidnapped New Orleans boy
___25. BOLLWEEVIL   Y. Jessie's dead father's cranky sister: Aunt ___

Slave Dancer Matching 3 Answer Key

A - 1. GALLEY	A. Where Curry prepared lentil soup
Q - 2. AFRICA	B. Used to try to clear stench from hold: chloride of ____
T - 3. GOLD	C. Corner of St. Louis and Chartres Streets: ___ Market
X - 4. JESSIE	D. Louisianian of French ancestry
D - 5. CREOLE	E. Carved on Jessie's mother's sewing box: ___ fish
J - 6. SHROUDS	F. Plea that served Jessie in the end: Oh ____!
B - 7. LIME	G. Cawthorne's first mate
G - 8. SPARK	H. Final destination of ship
H - 9. CHARLESTON	I. Jessie's father's French surname
V - 10. BEN	J. Ropes that support the mast
N - 11. BENIN	K. Captain's nickname for Jessie
R - 12. CANDLES	L. Defective black
E - 13. FLYING	M. Crescent-mouthed maggots with stitched teeth
U - 14. IBOS	N. African bay: Bight of ___
S - 15. BETTY	O. Black boy who survives with Jessie
L - 16. MACAROON	P. Slave woman Jessie saw in the Vieux Carre
F - 17. SWIM	Q. Where The Moonlight will pick up slaves
Y - 18. AGATHA	R. Needed by Jessie's mother to sew at night
C - 19. SLAVE	S. Jessie's sister
I - 20. BEAULIEU	T. Slave trade: Black ___
P - 21. STAR	U. Captain won't take any of them
W - 22. CAWTHORNE	V. Took Spark's place: ___ Stout
M - 23. SHARKS	W. Ship's captain
O - 24. RAS	X. Kidnapped New Orleans boy
K - 25. BOLLWEEVIL	Y. Jessie's dead father's cranky sister: Aunt ___

Slave Dancer Matching 4

___ 1. BENIN
___ 2. CARRE
___ 3. MOONLIGHT
___ 4. COCKROACH
___ 5. PRIVATEERS
___ 6. GOLD
___ 7. AGATHA
___ 8. LIME
___ 9. PURVIS
___ 10. CANDLES
___ 11. SHROUDS
___ 12. FLYING
___ 13. AFRICA
___ 14. REVENUE
___ 15. CRADLE
___ 16. BLOCKADE
___ 17. BOLLWEEVIL
___ 18. BETTY
___ 19. CASKS
___ 20. CHICKEN
___ 21. BOOM
___ 22. NEEDLE
___ 23. LOUT
___ 24. STAR
___ 25. CONGO

A. Needed by Jessie's mother to sew at night
B. Individuals profiting on slave trade
C. Carved on Jessie's mother's sewing box: ___ fish
D. Slaving ship: The ___
E. String game Purvis played with Jessie: Cat's ___
F. Slave trade: Black ___
G. First sign of life on deserted land
H. Used to try to clear stench from hold: chloride of ___
I. Object used to support Bollier family
J. Where The Moonlight will pick up slaves
K. Ropes that support the mast
L. Captain's nickname for Jessie
M. Slave woman Jessie saw in the Vieux Carre
N. New Orleans' French Quarter: Vieux ___
O. Jessie's dead father's cranky sister: Aunt ___
P. Patrols U.S. shores: U.S. ___ Cutters
Q. Kidnapper Jessie came to trust
R. Ras and Jessie hung onto it in the water
S. Jessie's sister
T. Oddly comforting sight upon Jessie's waking
U. African bay: Bight of ___
V. Aunt Agatha's name for Jessie: Bayou ___
W. Wooden kegs kept in the hold that held water
X. New Orleans spot for slave festivity: ___ Square
Y. Englishmen trying to stop slave trade: British ___

Slave Dancer Matching 4 Answer Key

U - 1. BENIN	A. Needed by Jessie's mother to sew at night
N - 2. CARRE	B. Individuals profiting on slave trade
D - 3. MOONLIGHT	C. Carved on Jessie's mother's sewing box: ___ fish
T - 4. COCKROACH	D. Slaving ship: The ___
B - 5. PRIVATEERS	E. String game Purvis played with Jessie: Cat's ___
F - 6. GOLD	F. Slave trade: Black ___
O - 7. AGATHA	G. First sign of life on deserted land
H - 8. LIME	H. Used to try to clear stench from hold: chloride of ___
Q - 9. PURVIS	I. Object used to support Bollier family
A - 10. CANDLES	J. Where The Moonlight will pick up slaves
K - 11. SHROUDS	K. Ropes that support the mast
C - 12. FLYING	L. Captain's nickname for Jessie
J - 13. AFRICA	M. Slave woman Jessie saw in the Vieux Carre
P - 14. REVENUE	N. New Orleans' French Quarter: Vieux ___
E - 15. CRADLE	O. Jessie's dead father's cranky sister: Aunt ___
Y - 16. BLOCKADE	P. Patrols U.S. shores: U.S. ___ Cutters
L - 17. BOLLWEEVIL	Q. Kidnapper Jessie came to trust
S - 18. BETTY	R. Ras and Jessie hung onto it in the water
W - 19. CASKS	S. Jessie's sister
G - 20. CHICKEN	T. Oddly comforting sight upon Jessie's waking
R - 21. BOOM	U. African bay: Bight of ___
I - 22. NEEDLE	V. Aunt Agatha's name for Jessie: Bayou ___
V - 23. LOUT	W. Wooden kegs kept in the hold that held water
M - 24. STAR	X. New Orleans spot for slave festivity: ___ Square
X - 25. CONGO	Y. Englishmen trying to stop slave trade: British ___

Slave Dancer Magic Squares 1

Match the definition with the vocabulary word. Put your answers in the magic squares below. When your answers are correct, all columns and rows will add to the same number.

A. BENIN
B. HOPE
C. MACAROON
D. CRADLE
E. CONGO
F. CREOLE
G. BLOCKADE
H. RAFT
I. HAMMOCK
J. CARRE
K. REVENUE
L. CAWTHORNE
M. NEEDLE
N. SHARKS
O. AGATHA
P. LOUT

1. Jessie's dead father's cranky sister: Aunt ___
2. New Orleans' French Quarter: Vieux ___
3. Craft on which Claudius and Purvis dumped Jessie
4. African bay: Bight of ___
5. String game Purvis played with Jessie: Cat's ___
6. New Orleans spot for slave festivity: ___ Square
7. Patrols U.S. shores: U.S. ___ Cutters
8. Crescent-mouthed maggots with stitched teeth
9. Louisianian of French ancestry
10. Defective black
11. Object used to support Bollier family
12. Ship's captain
13. Jessie's bed on ship
14. Aunt Agatha's name for Jessie: Bayou ___
15. Pushed Jessie on while dogpaddling
16. Englishmen trying to stop slave trade: British ___

A=	B=	C=	D=
E=	F=	G=	H=
I=	J=	K=	L=
M=	N=	O=	P=

Slave Dancer Magic Squares 1 Answer Key

Match the definition with the vocabulary word. Put your answers in the magic squares below. When your answers are correct, all columns and rows will add to the same number.

A. BENIN
B. HOPE
C. MACAROON
D. CRADLE
E. CONGO
F. CREOLE
G. BLOCKADE
H. RAFT
I. HAMMOCK
J. CARRE
K. REVENUE
L. CAWTHORNE
M. NEEDLE
N. SHARKS
O. AGATHA
P. LOUT

1. Jessie's dead father's cranky sister: Aunt ___
2. New Orleans' French Quarter: Vieux ___
3. Craft on which Claudius and Purvis dumped Jessie
4. African bay: Bight of ___
5. String game Purvis played with Jessie: Cat's ___
6. New Orleans spot for slave festivity: ___ Square
7. Patrols U.S. shores: U.S. ___ Cutters
8. Crescent-mouthed maggots with stitched teeth
9. Louisianian of French ancestry
10. Defective black
11. Object used to support Bollier family
12. Ship's captain
13. Jessie's bed on ship
14. Aunt Agatha's name for Jessie: Bayou ___
15. Pushed Jessie on while dogpaddling
16. Englishmen trying to stop slave trade: British ___

A=4	B=15	C=10	D=5
E=6	F=9	G=16	H=3
I=13	J=2	K=7	L=12
M=11	N=8	O=1	P=14

Slave Dancer Magic Squares 2

Match the definition with the vocabulary word. Put your answers in the magic squares below. When your answers are correct, all columns and rows will add to the same number.

A. LIME
B. BETTY
C. RAFT
D. NEEDLE
E. CRADLE
F. AGATHA
G. THIRTEEN
H. CHARLESTON
I. JESSIE
J. PRESSED
K. DANIEL
L. LOUT
M. APPRENTICE
N. NED
O. BOOM
P. BENIN

1. Used to try to clear stench from hold: chloride of ____
2. Ship's carpenter: ___ Grime
3. Pressganged or forced into ship's service
4. String game Purvis played with Jessie: Cat's ___
5. Slave dancer's age
6. Aunt Agatha's name for Jessie: Bayou ___
7. African bay: Bight of ___
8. Craft on which Claudius and Purvis dumped Jessie
9. Ras and Jessie hung onto it in the water
10. Object used to support Bollier family
11. Final destination of ship
12. Old Mississippi escaped black man who helps boys
13. Kidnapped New Orleans boy
14. Jessie's dead father's cranky sister: Aunt ___
15. Jessie's sister
16. Jessie did this under apothecary

A=	B=	C=	D=
E=	F=	G=	H=
I=	J=	K=	L=
M=	N=	O=	P=

Slave Dancer Magic Squares 2 Answer Key

Match the definition with the vocabulary word. Put your answers in the magic squares below. When your answers are correct, all columns and rows will add to the same number.

A. LIME
B. BETTY
C. RAFT
D. NEEDLE
E. CRADLE
F. AGATHA
G. THIRTEEN
H. CHARLESTON
I. JESSIE
J. PRESSED
K. DANIEL
L. LOUT
M. APPRENTICE
N. NED
O. BOOM
P. BENIN

1. Used to try to clear stench from hold: chloride of ____
2. Ship's carpenter: ___ Grime
3. Pressganged or forced into ship's service
4. String game Purvis played with Jessie: Cat's ___
5. Slave dancer's age
6. Aunt Agatha's name for Jessie: Bayou ___
7. African bay: Bight of ___
8. Craft on which Claudius and Purvis dumped Jessie
9. Ras and Jessie hung onto it in the water
10. Object used to support Bollier family
11. Final destination of ship
12. Old Mississippi escaped black man who helps boys
13. Kidnapped New Orleans boy
14. Jessie's dead father's cranky sister: Aunt ___
15. Jessie's sister
16. Jessie did this under apothecary

A=1	B=15	C=8	D=10
E=4	F=14	G=5	H=11
I=13	J=3	K=12	L=6
M=16	N=2	O=9	P=7

Slave Dancer Magic Squares 3

Match the definition with the vocabulary word. Put your answers in the magic squares below. When your answers are correct, all columns and rows will add to the same number.

A. CASKS
B. CAWTHORNE
C. GOLD
D. CREOLE
E. HAMMOCK
F. SHARKS
G. COCKROACH
H. LIME
I. BETTY
J. SHROUDS
K. SLAVE
L. NED
M. BLOCKADE
N. BOLLWEEVIL
O. RAS
P. STAR

1. Used to try to clear stench from hold: chloride of ____
2. Wooden kegs kept in the hold that held water
3. Ship's captain
4. Oddly comforting sight upon Jessie's waking
5. Ropes that support the mast
6. Black boy who survives with Jessie
7. Slave woman Jessie saw in the Vieux Carre
8. Jessie's sister
9. Corner of St. Louis and Chartres Streets: ___ Market
10. Captain's nickname for Jessie
11. Englishmen trying to stop slave trade: British ____
12. Ship's carpenter: ___ Grime
13. Jessie's bed on ship
14. Louisianian of French ancestry
15. Slave trade: Black ___
16. Crescent-mouthed maggots with stitched teeth

A=	B=	C=	D=
E=	F=	G=	H=
I=	J=	K=	L=
M=	N=	O=	P=

Slave Dancer Magic Squares 3 Answer Key

Match the definition with the vocabulary word. Put your answers in the magic squares below. When your answers are correct, all columns and rows will add to the same number.

A. CASKS
B. CAWTHORNE
C. GOLD
D. CREOLE
E. HAMMOCK
F. SHARKS
G. COCKROACH
H. LIME
I. BETTY
J. SHROUDS
K. SLAVE
L. NED
M. BLOCKADE
N. BOLLWEEVIL
O. RAS
P. STAR

1. Used to try to clear stench from hold: chloride of ____
2. Wooden kegs kept in the hold that held water
3. Ship's captain
4. Oddly comforting sight upon Jessie's waking
5. Ropes that support the mast
6. Black boy who survives with Jessie
7. Slave woman Jessie saw in the Vieux Carre
8. Jessie's sister
9. Corner of St. Louis and Chartres Streets: ____ Market
10. Captain's nickname for Jessie
11. Englishmen trying to stop slave trade: British ____
12. Ship's carpenter: ____ Grime
13. Jessie's bed on ship
14. Louisianian of French ancestry
15. Slave trade: Black ____
16. Crescent-mouthed maggots with stitched teeth

A=2	B=3	C=15	D=14
E=13	F=16	G=4	H=1
I=8	J=5	K=9	L=12
M=11	N=10	O=6	P=7

Slave Dancer Magic Squares 4

Match the definition with the vocabulary word. Put your answers in the magic squares below. When your answers are correct, all columns and rows will add to the same number.

A. GALLEY
B. FIFE
C. BOLLWEEVIL
D. MOONLIGHT
E. NED
F. GOLD
G. PRESSED
H. SHROUDS
I. FLYING
J. CREOLE
K. BOOM
L. PURVIS
M. COCKROACH
N. MACAROON
O. AFRICA
P. SPARK

1. Jessie's instrument
2. Pressganged or forced into ship's service
3. Ras and Jessie hung onto it in the water
4. Defective black
5. Oddly comforting sight upon Jessie's waking
6. Kidnapper Jessie came to trust
7. Ropes that support the mast
8. Where Curry prepared lentil soup
9. Cawthorne's first mate
10. Carved on Jessie's mother's sewing box: ___ fish
11. Ship's carpenter: ___ Grime
12. Slaving ship: The ___
13. Captain's nickname for Jessie
14. Slave trade: Black ___
15. Louisianian of French ancestry
16. Where The Moonlight will pick up slaves

A=	B=	C=	D=
E=	F=	G=	H=
I=	J=	K=	L=
M=	N=	O=	P=

Slave Dancer Magic Squares 4 Answer Key

Match the definition with the vocabulary word. Put your answers in the magic squares below. When your answers are correct, all columns and rows will add to the same number.

A. GALLEY
B. FIFE
C. BOLLWEEVIL
D. MOONLIGHT
E. NED
F. GOLD
G. PRESSED
H. SHROUDS
I. FLYING
J. CREOLE
K. BOOM
L. PURVIS
M. COCKROACH
N. MACAROON
O. AFRICA
P. SPARK

1. Jessie's instrument
2. Pressganged or forced into ship's service
3. Ras and Jessie hung onto it in the water
4. Defective black
5. Oddly comforting sight upon Jessie's waking
6. Kidnapper Jessie came to trust
7. Ropes that support the mast
8. Where Curry prepared lentil soup
9. Cawthorne's first mate
10. Carved on Jessie's mother's sewing box: ___ fish
11. Ship's carpenter: ___ Grime
12. Slaving ship: The ___
13. Captain's nickname for Jessie
14. Slave trade: Black ___
15. Louisianian of French ancestry
16. Where The Moonlight will pick up slaves

A=8	B=1	C=13	D=12
E=11	F=14	G=2	H=7
I=10	J=15	K=3	L=6
M=5	N=4	O=16	P=9

Slave Dancer Word Search 1

```
C R A D L E H H S R E E T A V I R P
H H S A I P M O I V R P C G T B J X
A B L N M F B B V D G J O N K E E B
R O A I E I C M R S B E N I N T S Y
L L V E G H I P U D P C G Y O T S F
E L E L I W B S P P X A O L O Y I C
S W N C S S C O X G H N R F R Y E X
T E K E D A K C O L B D Y K A H K P
O E S S C R J A Y M J L F W C A Q H
N V P H P T M W T G C E G N A M F F
N I R R K F Y T K M A S Y H M M V T
Y L E O M Z L H N S R L D O G O L D
A V S U Q C Q O K E R Q L P P C Z G
G X S D T F A R E V E N U E T K P P
A V E S W N A N T F L D L Y Y B T R
T N D G V H R E I N T O L C U R R Y
H L G G S H A F H L E N U E W V J M
A F R I C A S T A R N E E T R I H T
C U B A S K S A C B E A U L I E U F
```

African bay: Bight of ___ (5)
Aunt Agatha's name for Jessie: Bayou ___ (4)
Black boy who survives with Jessie (3)
Captain won't take any of them (4)
Captain's nickname for Jessie (10)
Carved on Jessie's mother's sewing box: ___ fish (6)
Cawthorne's first mate (5)
Corner of St. Louis and Chartres Streets: ___ Market (5)
Craft on which Claudius and Purvis dumped Jessie (4)
Crescent-mouthed maggots with stitched teeth (6)
Defective black (8)
Englishmen trying to stop slave trade: British ___ (8)
Final destination of ship (10)
First sign of life on deserted land (7)
Individuals profiting on slave trade (10)
Jessie's bed on ship (7)
Jessie's dead father's cranky sister: Aunt ___ (6)
Jessie's father's French surname (8)
Jessie's instrument (4)
Jessie's sister (5)
Kidnapped New Orleans boy (6)
Kidnapper Jessie came to trust (6)
Louisianian of French ancestry (6)

Needed by Jessie's mother to sew at night (7)
New Orleans spot for slave festivity: ___ Square (5)
New Orleans' French Quarter: Vieux ___ (5)
Object used to support Bollier family (6)
Old Mississippi escaped black man who helps boys (6)
Patrols U.S. shores: U.S. ___ Cutters
Place where slaves will be sold (4)
Plea that served Jessie in the end: Oh ___! (4)
Pressganged or forced into ship's service (7)
Pushed Jessie on while dogpaddling (4)
Ras and Jessie hung onto it in the water (4)
Ropes that support the mast (7)
Ship's captain (9)
Ship's carpenter: ___ Grime (3)
Ship's cook (5)
Slave dancer's age (8)
Slave trade: Black ___ (4)
Slave woman Jessie saw in the Vieux Carre (4)
String game Purvis played with Jessie: Cat's ___ (6)
Took Spark's place: ___ Stout (3)
Used to try to clear stench from hold: chloride of ___ (4)
Where Curry prepared lentil soup (6)
Where The Moonlight will pick up slaves (6)
Wooden kegs kept in the hold that held water (5)

Slave Dancer Word Search 1 Answer Key

```
C R A D L E       S R E E T A V I R P
H   S A I     O   I       C   G     B   J
A   B L N M   B   V       O   N     E   E
R   O A I   C   M R   S   B   I   N T   S
L   L L E   H I     U   P   C   O   T   S
E   L E L W B     P   A   G   O   Y   I
S   W   C S     O     N   O   F     R   E
T   E K E D A K C O L B   D   K   H
O   E   S       A   M   L       A
N   V P H       W   G   C       C
    I R R       T       A   S   H
    L E O       H   N S R   L   O       G O L D
A   S U         O   K E R   L   P       C
G   S D   T F A R E V E N U E   K
A   E S         A   N     F     L Y
T N     D         H R E I       O L C U R R Y
H         S         A F         L U
A F R I C A S T A R N E E T R I H T
C U B A S K S A C B E A U L I E U
```

African bay: Bight of ___ (5)
Aunt Agatha's name for Jessie: Bayou ___ (4)
Black boy who survives with Jessie (3)
Captain won't take any of them (4)
Captain's nickname for Jessie (10)
Carved on Jessie's mother's sewing box: ___ fish (6)
Cawthorne's first mate (5)
Corner of St. Louis and Chartres Streets: ___ Market (5)
Craft on which Claudius and Purvis dumped Jessie (4)
Crescent-mouthed maggots with stitched teeth (6)
Defective black (8)
Englishmen trying to stop slave trade: British ____ (8)
Final destination of ship (10)
First sign of life on deserted land (7)
Individuals profiting on slave trade (10)
Jessie's bed on ship (7)
Jessie's dead father's cranky sister: Aunt ___ (6)
Jessie's father's French surname (8)
Jessie's instrument (4)
Jessie's sister (5)
Kidnapped New Orleans boy (6)
Kidnapper Jessie came to trust (6)
Louisianian of French ancestry (6)

Needed by Jessie's mother to sew at night (7)
New Orleans spot for slave festivity: ___ Square (5)
New Orleans' French Quarter: Vieux ____ (5)
Object used to support Bollier family (6)
Old Mississippi escaped black man who helps boys (6)
Patrols U.S. shores: U.S. ___ Cutters
Place where slaves will be sold (4)
Plea that served Jessie in the end: Oh ____! (4)
Pressganged or forced into ship's service (7)
Pushed Jessie on while dogpaddling (4)
Ras and Jessie hung onto it in the water (4)
Ropes that support the mast (7)
Ship's captain (9)
Ship's carpenter: ___ Grime (3)
Ship's cook (5)
Slave dancer's age (8)
Slave trade: Black ___ (4)
Slave woman Jessie saw in the Vieux Carre (4)
String game Purvis played with Jessie: Cat's ___ (6)
Took Spark's place: ___ Stout (3)
Used to try to clear stench from hold: chloride of ____ (4)
Where Curry prepared lentil soup (6)
Where The Moonlight will pick up slaves (6)
Wooden kegs kept in the hold that held water (5)

Slave Dancer Word Search 2

```
C A N D L E S S C U R R Y B H N C V
Q P R E S S E D B E T T Y S E O E F
M U V L C J L U A D Q S O F N N P D
M R A V H O F O H N F B I G K J I E
C V W T G C A R R E I F O C L E C N
E I L S Q H R H M S H E O S M S H N
A S O T T A E S R K V M L I I S I R
G Z U A H R V V R M B L Z W I C J
A Q T R I L E L D A R C B C S E K K
T P A G R E N B H H F O L N A H E C
H S P F T S U E P S O T O E M S N C
A W A R E T E N P M K F C E O G K Q
C Z F S E O B N M C V L K D O Q R S
Y Z R T N N H W K R H Y A L N R N Z
X H I M P C T F V E L I D E L S Z G
W K C U B A B I M O Z N E G I P Y D
H C A O R K C O C L L G Y C G A F M
J W C B O L L W E E V I L J H R G S
B E A U L I E U G A L L E Y T K N N
```

African bay: Bight of ____ (5)
Aunt Agatha's name for Jessie: Bayou ____ (4)
Black boy who survives with Jessie (3)
Captain won't take any of them (4)
Captain's nickname for Jessie (10)
Carved on Jessie's mother's sewing box: ____ fish (6)
Cawthorne's first mate (5)
Corner of St. Louis and Chartres Streets: ____ Market (5)
Craft on which Claudius and Purvis dumped Jessie (4)
Crescent-mouthed maggots with stitched teeth (6)
Englishmen trying to stop slave trade: British ____ (8)
Final destination of ship (10)
First sign of life on deserted land (7)
Jessie did this under apothecary (10)
Jessie's bed on ship (7)
Jessie's dead father's cranky sister: Aunt ____ (6)
Jessie's father's French surname (8)
Jessie's instrument (4)
Jessie's sister (5)
Kidnapped New Orleans boy (6)
Kidnapper Jessie came to trust (6)
Louisianian of French ancestry (6)
Needed by Jessie's mother to sew at night (7)

New Orleans spot for slave festivity: ____ Square (5)
New Orleans' French Quarter: Vieux ____ (5)
Object used to support Bollier family (6)
Oddly comforting sight upon Jessie's waking (9)
Old Mississippi escaped black man who helps boys (6)
Patrols U.S. shores: U.S. ____ Cutters
Place where slaves will be sold (4)
Plea that served Jessie in the end: Oh ____! (4)
Pressganged or forced into ship's service (7)
Pushed Jessie on while dogpaddling (4)
Ras and Jessie hung onto it in the water (4)
Ropes that support the mast (7)
Ship's carpenter: ____ Grime (3)
Ship's cook (5)
Slave dancer's age (8)
Slave trade: Black ____ (4)
Slave woman Jessie saw in the Vieux Carre (4)
Slaving ship: The ____ (9)
String game Purvis played with Jessie: Cat's ____ (6)
Took Spark's place: ____ Stout (3)
Used to try to clear stench from hold: chloride of ____ (4)
Where Curry prepared lentil soup (6)
Where The Moonlight will pick up slaves (6)
Wooden kegs kept in the hold that held water (5)

Slave Dancer Word Search 2 Answer Key

```
C A N D L E S S C U R R Y B H N C
  P R E S S E D B E T T Y S E O E
  U L     L     U A     O F N N P   D
  R A     O     O N     B I G K J   E
  V     G C A R R E I F O C E C   N
E I L S   H H   S   E O   M S H
A S O T   A E   K   E     I S I
G   U A   R V   R M   B C W E C
A   T R   I L D A R C O L S A   K
T P A     R N B   H F L N   M   E
H S P     T S U   S O E E   S   N
A   A     E E N   O M C E       K
    F         O     C L K D       S
    R         N     R Y A E
    I                 E I D E
    C U B A       T   O N E
H C A O R K C O L     G L     S
    B O L L W E E V I L H     P
B E A U L I E U G A L L E Y T R K
```

African bay: Bight of ___ (5)
Aunt Agatha's name for Jessie: Bayou ___ (4)
Black boy who survives with Jessie (3)
Captain won't take any of them (4)
Captain's nickname for Jessie (10)
Carved on Jessie's mother's sewing box: ___ fish (6)
Cawthorne's first mate (5)
Corner of St. Louis and Chartres Streets: ___ Market (5)
Craft on which Claudius and Purvis dumped Jessie (4)
Crescent-mouthed maggots with stitched teeth (6)
Englishmen trying to stop slave trade: British ___ (8)
Final destination of ship (10)
First sign of life on deserted land (7)
Jessie did this under apothecary (10)
Jessie's bed on ship (7)
Jessie's dead father's cranky sister: Aunt ___ (6)
Jessie's father's French surname (8)
Jessie's instrument (4)
Jessie's sister (5)
Kidnapped New Orleans boy (6)
Kidnapper Jessie came to trust (6)
Louisianian of French ancestry (6)
Needed by Jessie's mother to sew at night (7)

New Orleans spot for slave festivity: ___ Square (5)
New Orleans' French Quarter: Vieux ___ (5)
Object used to support Bollier family (6)
Oddly comforting sight upon Jessie's waking (9)
Old Mississippi escaped black man who helps boys (6)
Patrols U.S. shores: U.S. ___ Cutters
Place where slaves will be sold (4)
Plea that served Jessie in the end: Oh ___! (4)
Pressganged or forced into ship's service (7)
Pushed Jessie on while dogpaddling (4)
Ras and Jessie hung onto it in the water (4)
Ropes that support the mast (7)
Ship's carpenter: ___ Grime (3)
Ship's cook (5)
Slave dancer's age (8)
Slave trade: Black ___ (4)
Slave woman Jessie saw in the Vieux Carre (4)
Slaving ship: The ___ (9)
String game Purvis played with Jessie: Cat's ___ (6)
Took Spark's place: ___ Stout (3)
Used to try to clear stench from hold: chloride of ___ (4)
Where Curry prepared lentil soup (6)
Where The Moonlight will pick up slaves (6)
Wooden kegs kept in the hold that held water (5)

Slave Dancer Word Search 3

```
T P N S C O C K R O A C H P X S N T
H Z O H T H G I L N O M Y R V K Q D
I B O R Q X I V D D F L R I N G X N
R N R O K G V E Q T A C V V W O Z
T L A K P A E T K M C H A L T F M
E Z C D L U N G J E O I T S X W J
E R A S H R K S L N N E B K N B
N Y M Y H P O V V B G J L E S J
N L K O L P H S I J R X R X J F
M N P N G R T L Z S A G C P C E R
B E T T Y E W V O H S P R K E S S
S D J C Z N A S C U Y N R L E S R
P C N B L T C E J W T V R D L S I K
B R A F T I C U B A Q Y E D Y E K K
O A E P F C M N G F G E N I L Y F
D D S S F E M E O R N A R F O M W D
M L T F S I H V L I C U T E I H O S
H E A H W E F E D C C L R H F W Q
K J R S Q W D R P A K C R C A P E
```

AFRICA
AGATHA
APPRENTICE
BEN
BENIN
BETTY
BOOM
CANDLES
CARRE
CASKS
CAWTHORNE
CHARLESTON

CHICKEN
COCKROACH
CONGO
CRADLE
CREOLE
CUBA
CURRY
DANIEL
FIFE
FLYING
GALLEY
GOLD

HOPE
IBOS
JESSIE
LIME
LOUT
MACAROON
MOONLIGHT
NED
NEEDLE
PRESSED
PRIVATEERS
PURVIS

RAFT
RAS
REVENUE
SHARKS
SHROUDS
SLAVE
SPARK
STAR
SWIM
THIRTEEN

Slave Dancer Word Search 3 Answer Key

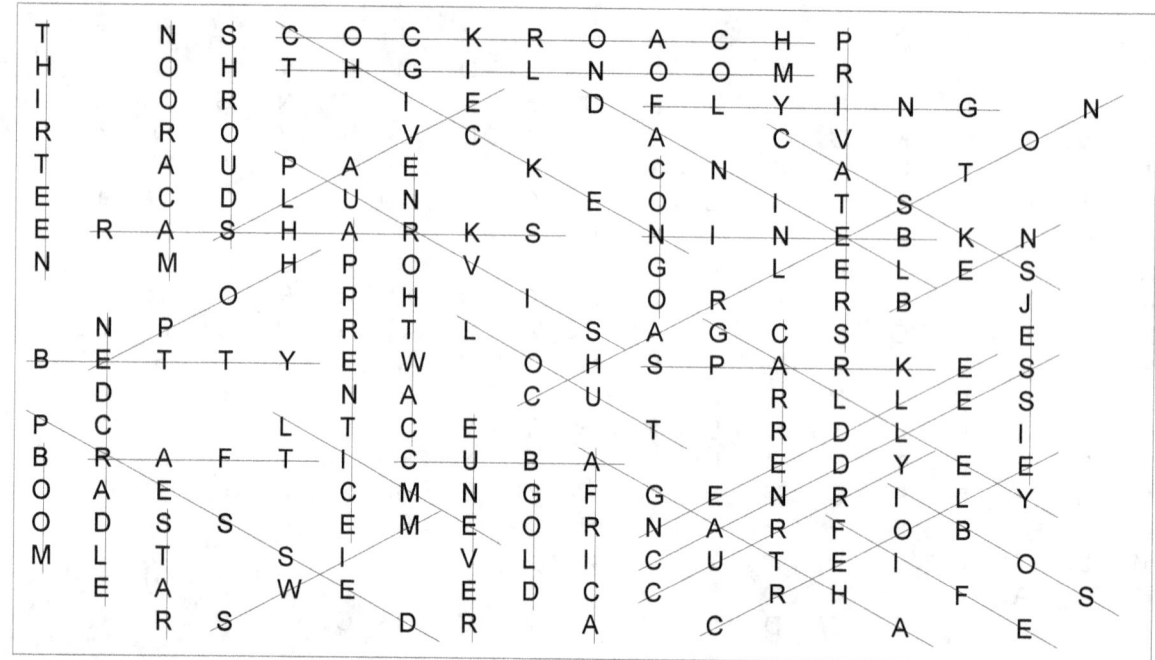

AFRICA	CHICKEN	HOPE	RAFT
AGATHA	COCKROACH	IBOS	RAS
APPRENTICE	CONGO	JESSIE	REVENUE
BEN	CRADLE	LIME	SHARKS
BENIN	CREOLE	LOUT	SHROUDS
BETTY	CUBA	MACAROON	SLAVE
BOOM	CURRY	MOONLIGHT	SPARK
CANDLES	DANIEL	NED	STAR
CARRE	FIFE	NEEDLE	SWIM
CASKS	FLYING	PRESSED	THIRTEEN
CAWTHORNE	GALLEY	PRIVATEERS	
CHARLESTON	GOLD	PURVIS	

Slave Dancer Word Search 4

```
G A L L E Y N C T K G Z F P S D C S
F Y N E D L F Z U Q C L T T H A H W
K C O M L A M O B I Q R O R A N A Z
B C O G A H D L V A C P O G U I R C
Y E B A P P K T E L C E P N D E L Z
R A T S D G U T Q R A A A F S L E S
M H J T S O W R H Z F N P E A E S D
A Z B Y Y L R G V A G C R U C S T D
P C H O O D I A D I S B E N I N O M
R I A O L X L F K E M N T R N E N M
I B B W L M E E R T I S V E F E O W
V O L O N V A F N S H I E F E T R G
A S O O T P B L L S A C R M R R A Y
T M W O C H O Y F L R E G U I I C N
E L R I R S R I T V K X C F H H A N
E C Q C M K A N G E S C G N T M M R
R J E S U V I E D G E E D J Z K F Q
S K A A C V P R C H I C K E N J Y S
B E A U L I E U E S K E N J Y F S F
```

AFRICA	CAWTHORNE	HAMMOCK	RAFT
AGATHA	CHARLESTON	HOPE	RAS
APPRENTICE	CHICKEN	IBOS	REVENUE
BEAULIEU	CONGO	JESSIE	SHARKS
BEN	CRADLE	LIME	SHROUDS
BENIN	CREOLE	LOUT	SLAVE
BETTY	CUBA	MACAROON	SPARK
BLOCKADE	CURRY	MOONLIGHT	STAR
BOLLWEEVIL	DANIEL	NED	SWIM
BOOM	FIFE	NEEDLE	THIRTEEN
CANDLES	FLYING	PRESSED	
CARRE	GALLEY	PRIVATEERS	
CASKS	GOLD	PURVIS	

Slave Dancer Word Search 4 Answer Key

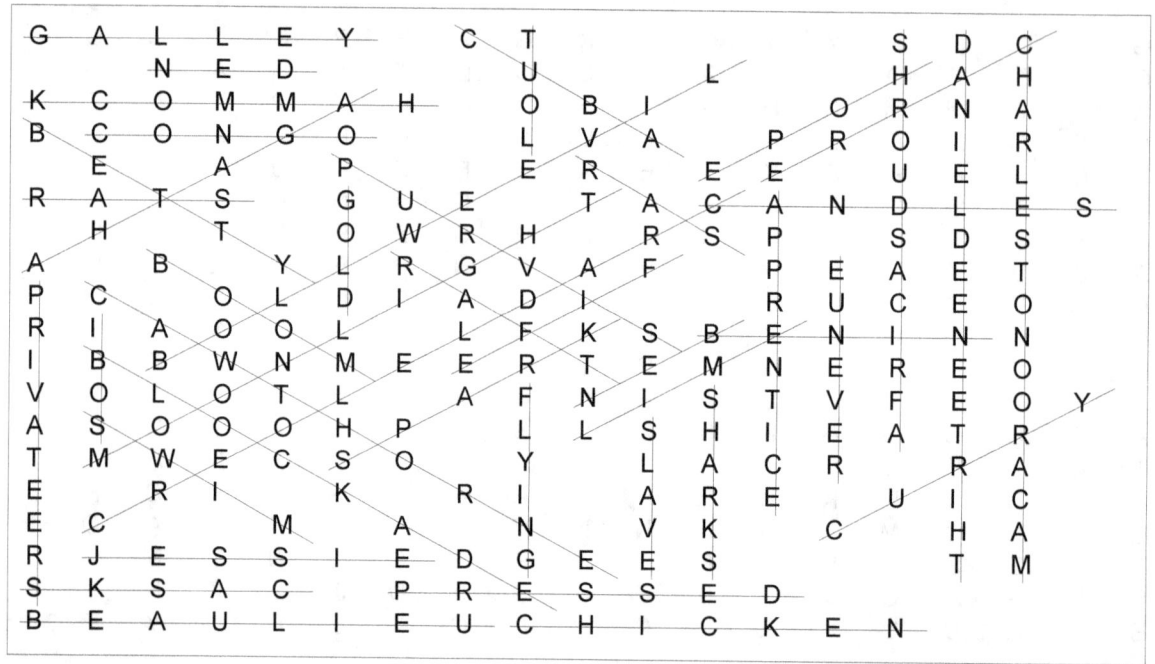

AFRICA	CAWTHORNE	HAMMOCK	RAFT
AGATHA	CHARLESTON	HOPE	RAS
APPRENTICE	CHICKEN	IBOS	REVENUE
BEAULIEU	CONGO	JESSIE	SHARKS
BEN	CRADLE	LIME	SHROUDS
BENIN	CREOLE	LOUT	SLAVE
BETTY	CUBA	MACAROON	SPARK
BLOCKADE	CURRY	MOONLIGHT	STAR
BOLLWEEVIL	DANIEL	NED	SWIM
BOOM	FIFE	NEEDLE	THIRTEEN
CANDLES	FLYING	PRESSED	
CARRE	GALLEY	PRIVATEERS	
CASKS	GOLD	PURVIS	

Slave Dancer Crossword 1

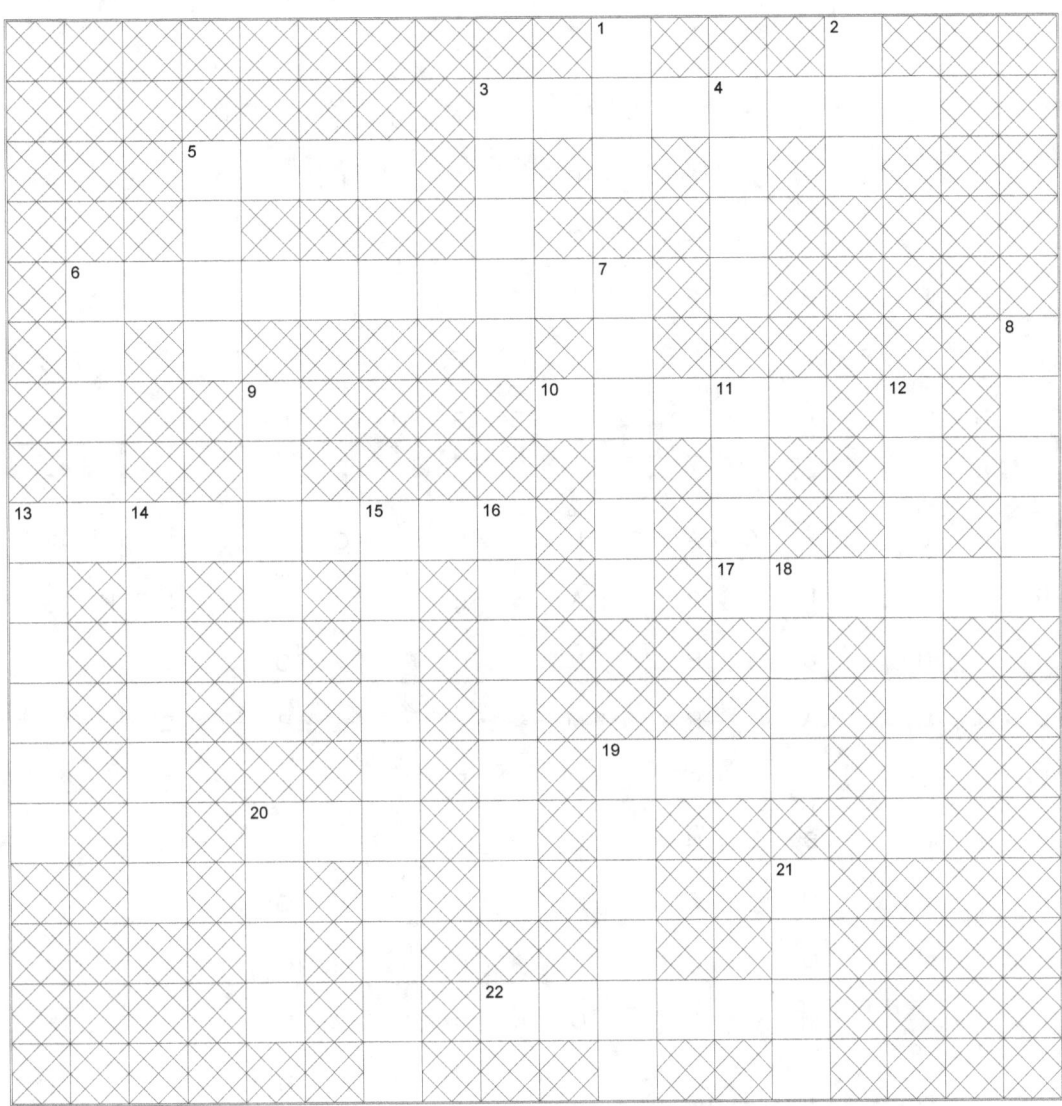

Across
3. Jessie's father's French surname
5. Plea that served Jessie in the end: Oh ____!
6. Final destination of ship
10. African bay: Bight of ___
13. Oddly comforting sight upon Jessie's waking
17. Crescent-mouthed maggots with stitched teeth
19. Jessie's instrument
20. Took Spark's place: ___ Stout
22. Old Mississippi escaped black man who helps boys

Down
1. Black boy who survives with Jessie
2. Ship's carpenter: ___ Grime
3. Jessie's sister
4. Used to try to clear stench from hold: chloride of ____
5. Slave woman Jessie saw in the Vieux Carre
6. New Orleans spot for slave festivity: ___ Square
7. Object used to support Bollier family
8. Wooden kegs kept in the hold that held water
9. Where The Moonlight will pick up slaves
11. Captain won't take any of them
12. Slave dancer's age
13. String game Purvis played with Jessie: Cat's ___
14. Needed by Jessie's mother to sew at night
15. Jessie did this under apothecary
16. Jessie's bed on ship
18. Pushed Jessie on while dogpaddling
19. Carved on Jessie's mother's sewing box: ___ fish
20. Ras and Jessie hung onto it in the water
21. Slave trade: Black ___

Slave Dancer Crossword 1 Answer Key

							1 R		2 N		
					3 B	E	A U	4 L	I E	U	
		5 S	W	I	M		E	A		I		D
		T					T			M		
	6 C	H	A	R	L	E	S	T	7 O	N		E
	O		R						Y		E		8 C
	N			9 A			10 B	E	11 N	I	N	12 T	A
	G			F				D		B		H	S
13 C	O	14 C	K	R	15 O	A	16 C	H	L		O		I	K
R		A		I		P		P	A		17 S	18 H	A	R	K	S
A		N		C		P		M			O		T		E
D		D		A		R		M		19 F	I	F	E		E
L		L				E		O						N
E		E		20 B	E	N		C		L				
		S		O		T		K		Y		21 G		
				O		I				I		O		
				M		C		22 D	A	N	I	E	L	
				E				G				D		

Across
3. Jessie's father's French surname
5. Plea that served Jessie in the end: Oh ____!
6. Final destination of ship
10. African bay: Bight of ___
13. Oddly comforting sight upon Jessie's waking
17. Crescent-mouthed maggots with stitched teeth
19. Jessie's instrument
20. Took Spark's place: ___ Stout
22. Old Mississippi escaped black man who helps boys

Down
1. Black boy who survives with Jessie
2. Ship's carpenter: ___ Grime
3. Jessie's sister
4. Used to try to clear stench from hold: chloride of ____
5. Slave woman Jessie saw in the Vieux Carre
6. New Orleans spot for slave festivity: ___ Square
7. Object used to support Bollier family
8. Wooden kegs kept in the hold that held water
9. Where The Moonlight will pick up slaves
11. Captain won't take any of them
12. Slave dancer's age
13. String game Purvis played with Jessie: Cat's ___
14. Needed by Jessie's mother to sew at night
15. Jessie did this under apothecary
16. Jessie's bed on ship
18. Pushed Jessie on while dogpaddling
19. Carved on Jessie's mother's sewing box: ___ fish
20. Ras and Jessie hung onto it in the water
21. Slave trade: Black ___

Slave Dancer Crossword 2

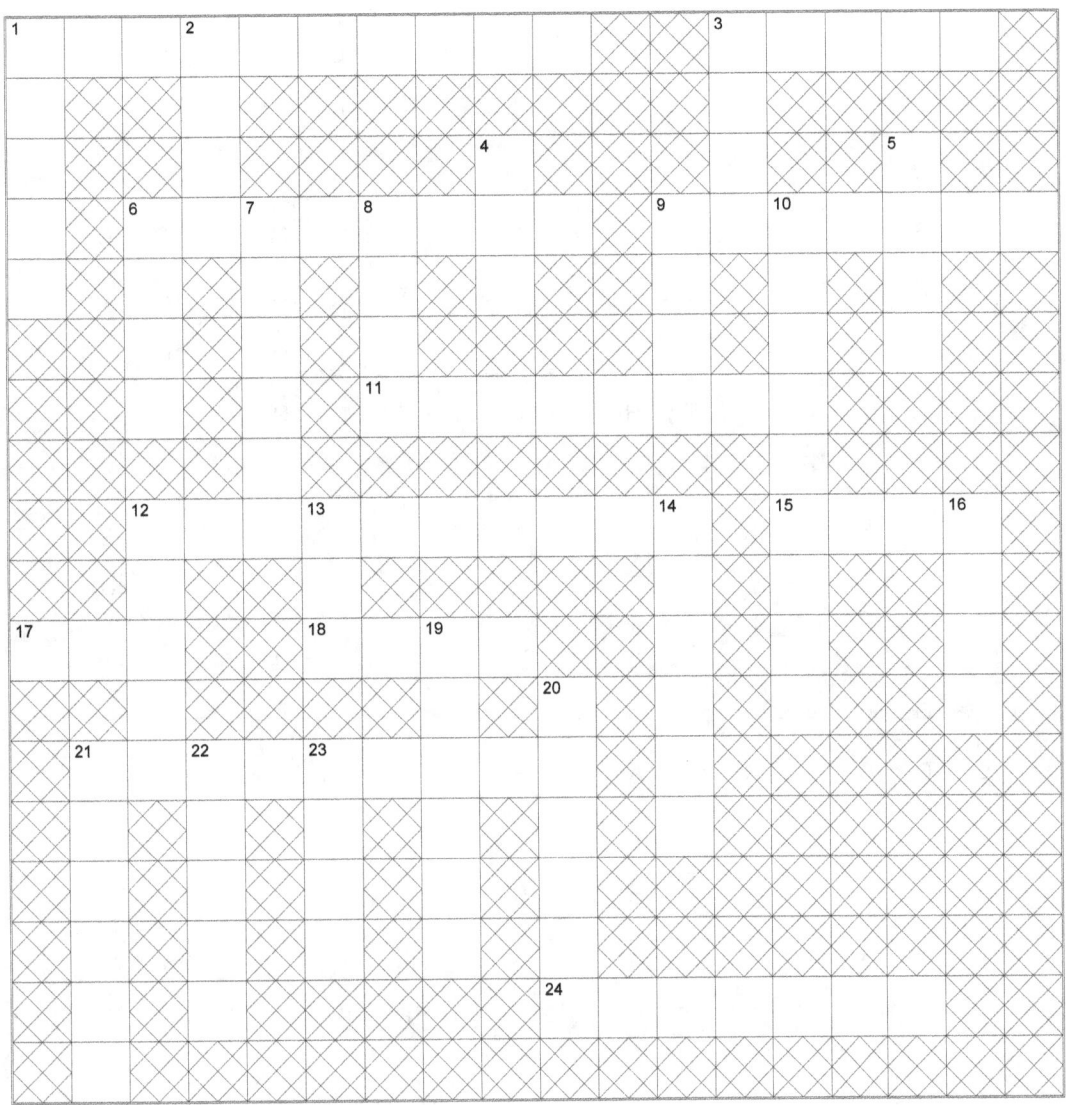

Across
1. Captain's nickname for Jessie
3. Ship's cook
6. Jessie's father's French surname
9. Jessie's bed on ship
11. Slave dancer's age
12. Final destination of ship
15. Captain won't take any of them
17. Took Spark's place: ___ Stout
18. Slave woman Jessie saw in the Vieux Carre
21. Oddly comforting sight upon Jessie's waking
24. Ropes that support the mast

Down
1. Jessie's sister
2. Used to try to clear stench from hold: chloride of ____
3. Place where slaves will be sold
4. Ship's carpenter: ___ Grime
5. Slave trade: Black ___
6. Ras and Jessie hung onto it in the water
7. Where The Moonlight will pick up slaves
8. Aunt Agatha's name for Jessie: Bayou ___
9. Pushed Jessie on while dogpaddling
10. Slaving ship: The ___
12. New Orleans spot for slave festivity: ___ Square
13. Black boy who survives with Jessie
14. Object used to support Bollier family
16. Plea that served Jessie in the end: Oh ____!
19. Jessie's dead father's cranky sister: Aunt ___
20. Crescent-mouthed maggots with stitched teeth
21. String game Purvis played with Jessie: Cat's ___
22. Wooden kegs kept in the hold that held water
23. Craft on which Claudius and Purvis dumped Jessie

Slave Dancer Crossword 2 Answer Key

	1 B	O	L	2 L	W	E	E	V	I	L		3 C	U	R	R	Y
	E			I								U				
	T			M				4 N				B		5 G		
	T		6 B	E	7 A	U	8 L	I	E	U		9 H	10 A	M	M	O	C	K
	Y		O		F		O		D			O		O		L		
			O		R		U					P		O		D		
			M		I		11 T	H	I	R	T	E	E	N				
					C									L				
			12 C	H	13 A	R	L	E	S	T	O	14 N	15 I	B	O	16 S
			O		A							E		G		W
	17 B	E	N		18 S	T	19 A	R			E		H		I
			G				G	20 S	D		T		M
			21 C	O	22 C	K	23 R	O	A	C	H	L			
			R		A		A		T		A	E			
			A		S		F		H		R				
			D		K		T		A		K				
			L		S			24 S	H	R	O	U	D	S
			E											

Across
1. Captain's nickname for Jessie
3. Ship's cook
6. Jessie's father's French surname
9. Jessie's bed on ship
11. Slave dancer's age
12. Final destination of ship
15. Captain won't take any of them
17. Took Spark's place: ___ Stout
18. Slave woman Jessie saw in the Vieux Carre
21. Oddly comforting sight upon Jessie's waking
24. Ropes that support the mast

Down
1. Jessie's sister
2. Used to try to clear stench from hold: chloride of ____
3. Place where slaves will be sold
4. Ship's carpenter: ___ Grime
5. Slave trade: Black ___
6. Ras and Jessie hung onto it in the water
7. Where The Moonlight will pick up slaves
8. Aunt Agatha's name for Jessie: Bayou ___
9. Pushed Jessie on while dogpaddling
10. Slaving ship: The ___
12. New Orleans spot for slave festivity: ___ Square
13. Black boy who survives with Jessie
14. Object used to support Bollier family
16. Plea that served Jessie in the end: Oh ___!
19. Jessie's dead father's cranky sister: Aunt ___
20. Crescent-mouthed maggots with stitched teeth
21. String game Purvis played with Jessie: Cat's ___
22. Wooden kegs kept in the hold that held water
23. Craft on which Claudius and Purvis dumped Jessie

Slave Dancer Crossword 3

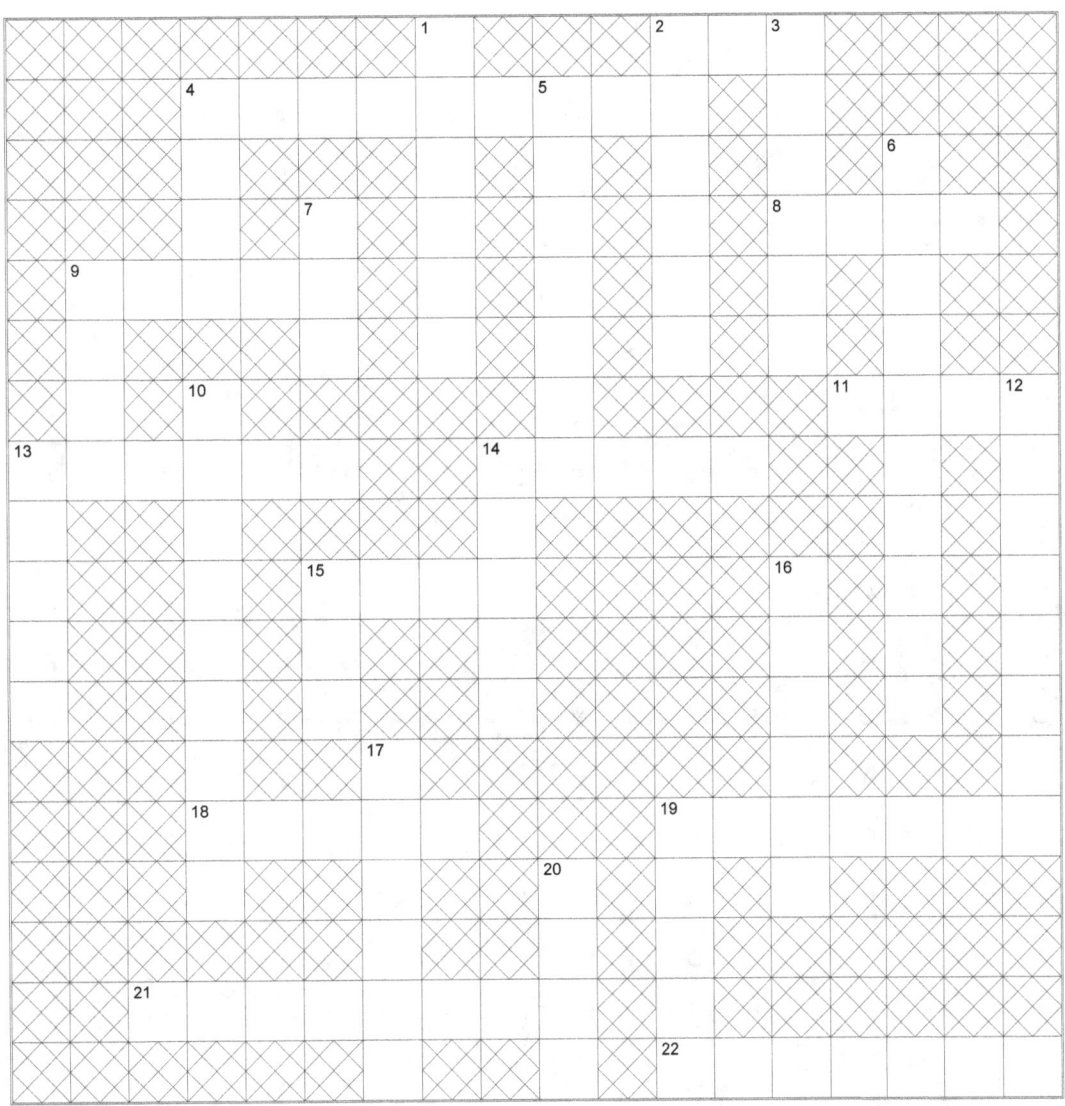

Across
2. Ship's carpenter: ___ Grime
4. Ship's captain
8. Captain won't take any of them
9. Corner of St. Louis and Chartres Streets: ___ Market
11. Plea that served Jessie in the end: Oh ____!
13. Louisianian of French ancestry
14. African bay: Bight of ___
15. Craft on which Claudius and Purvis dumped Jessie
18. New Orleans' French Quarter: Vieux ____
19. First sign of life on deserted land
21. Jessie's father's French surname
22. Ropes that support the mast

Down
1. Crescent-mouthed maggots with stitched teeth
2. Object used to support Bollier family
3. Old Mississippi escaped black man who helps boys
4. Place where slaves will be sold
5. Patrols U.S. shores: U.S. ___ Cutters
6. Captain's nickname for Jessie
7. Took Spark's place: ___ Stout
9. Slave woman Jessie saw in the Vieux Carre
10. Oddly comforting sight upon Jessie's waking
12. Defective black
13. New Orleans spot for slave festivity: ___ Square
14. Jessie's sister
15. Black boy who survives with Jessie
16. Kidnapper Jessie came to trust
17. String game Purvis played with Jessie: Cat's ___
19. Wooden kegs kept in the hold that held water
20. Aunt Agatha's name for Jessie: Bayou ___

Slave Dancer Crossword 3 Answer Key

						¹S			²N	E	³D		
		⁴C	A	W	T	H	O	⁵R	N	E	A		
		U				A		E	E		N		⁶B
		B		⁷B		R		V	E		⁸I	B	O	S
	⁹S	L	A	V	E		K		E		L	E	L
	T			N			S		N		E	L	L
	A		¹⁰C						U		¹¹S	W	I	¹²M
¹³C	R	E	O	L	E		¹⁴B	E	N	I	N		E	A
O			C				E						E	C
N			K		¹⁵R	A	F	T			¹⁶P		V	A
G			R		A		T				U		I	R
O			O		S		Y				R		L	O
			A		¹⁷C						V			O
		¹⁸C	A	R	R	E			¹⁹C	H	I	C	K	E	N
		H			A		²⁰L		A		S			
		D					O		S					
	²¹B	E	A	U	L	I	E	U		K				
		E					T		²²S	H	R	O	U	D	S

Across
2. Ship's carpenter: ___ Grime
4. Ship's captain
8. Captain won't take any of them
9. Corner of St. Louis and Chartres Streets: ___ Market
11. Plea that served Jessie in the end: Oh ____!
13. Louisianian of French ancestry
14. African bay: Bight of ___
15. Craft on which Claudius and Purvis dumped Jessie
18. New Orleans' French Quarter: Vieux ____
19. First sign of life on deserted land
21. Jessie's father's French surname
22. Ropes that support the mast

Down
1. Crescent-mouthed maggots with stitched teeth
2. Object used to support Bollier family
3. Old Mississippi escaped black man who helps boys
4. Place where slaves will be sold
5. Patrols U.S. shores: U.S. ___ Cutters
6. Captain's nickname for Jessie
7. Took Spark's place: ___ Stout
9. Slave woman Jessie saw in the Vieux Carre
10. Oddly comforting sight upon Jessie's waking
12. Defective black
13. New Orleans spot for slave festivity: ___ Square
14. Jessie's sister
15. Black boy who survives with Jessie
16. Kidnapper Jessie came to trust
17. String game Purvis played with Jessie: Cat's ___
19. Wooden kegs kept in the hold that held water
20. Aunt Agatha's name for Jessie: Bayou ___

Slave Dancer Crossword 4

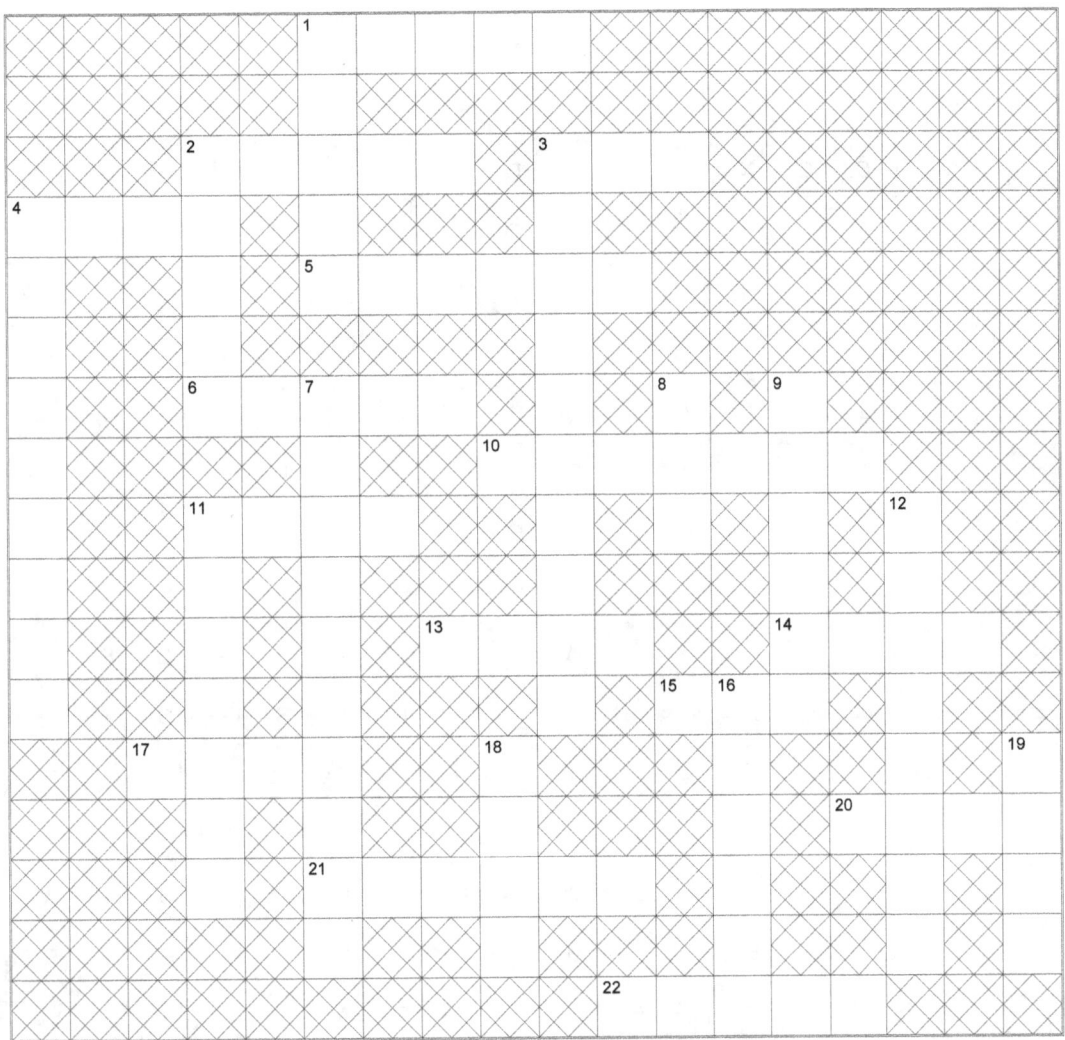

Across
1. Jessie's sister
2. New Orleans spot for slave festivity: ___ Square
3. Took Spark's place: ___ Stout
4. Place where slaves will be sold
5. Object used to support Bollier family
6. Corner of St. Louis and Chartres Streets: ___ Market
10. Patrols U.S. shores: U.S. ___ Cutters
11. Pushed Jessie on while dogpaddling
13. Plea that served Jessie in the end: Oh ____!
14. Captain won't take any of them
15. Black boy who survives with Jessie
17. Aunt Agatha's name for Jessie: Bayou ___
20. Craft on which Claudius and Purvis dumped Jessie
21. Louisianian of French ancestry
22. Cawthorne's first mate

Down
1. African bay: Bight of ___
2. Wooden kegs kept in the hold that held water
3. Captain's nickname for Jessie
4. Ship's captain
7. Jessie did this under apothecary
8. Ship's carpenter: ___ Grime
9. Kidnapper Jessie came to trust
11. Jessie's bed on ship
12. Englishmen trying to stop slave trade: British ____
16. Where The Moonlight will pick up slaves
18. Ras and Jessie hung onto it in the water
19. Slave woman Jessie saw in the Vieux Carre

Slave Dancer Crossword 4 Answer Key

Across
1. Jessie's sister
2. New Orleans spot for slave festivity: ___ Square
3. Took Spark's place: ___ Stout
4. Place where slaves will be sold
5. Object used to support Bollier family
6. Corner of St. Louis and Chartres Streets: ___ Market
10. Patrols U.S. shores: U.S. ___ Cutters
11. Pushed Jessie on while dogpaddling
13. Plea that served Jessie in the end: Oh ____!
14. Captain won't take any of them
15. Black boy who survives with Jessie
17. Aunt Agatha's name for Jessie: Bayou ___
20. Craft on which Claudius and Purvis dumped Jessie
21. Louisianian of French ancestry
22. Cawthorne's first mate

Down
1. African bay: Bight of ___
2. Wooden kegs kept in the hold that held water
3. Captain's nickname for Jessie
4. Ship's captain
7. Jessie did this under apothecary
8. Ship's carpenter: ___ Grime
9. Kidnapper Jessie came to trust
11. Jessie's bed on ship
12. Englishmen trying to stop slave trade: British ____
16. Where The Moonlight will pick up slaves
18. Ras and Jessie hung onto it in the water
19. Slave woman Jessie saw in the Vieux Carre

Slave Dancer

COCKROACH	SHROUDS	LOUT	AGATHA	SLAVE
CANDLES	PURVIS	HOPE	CREOLE	CUBA
PRIVATEERS	BOLLWEEVIL	FREE SPACE	SPARK	FIFE
BENIN	CURRY	CRADLE	THIRTEEN	IBOS
REVENUE	GOLD	NED	BEAULIEU	CARRE

Slave Dancer

PRESSED	CASKS	FLYING	BLOCKADE	AFRICA
MACAROON	BETTY	JESSIE	NEEDLE	BEN
MOONLIGHT	CONGO	FREE SPACE	CHICKEN	DANIEL
BOOM	RAS	STAR	GALLEY	APPRENTICE
SWIM	CAWTHORNE	LIME	RAFT	SHARKS

Slave Dancer

FLYING	AGATHA	CUBA	NED	BOOM
NEEDLE	SWIM	LOUT	LIME	CARRE
BETTY	CURRY	FREE SPACE	PRIVATEERS	DANIEL
CHICKEN	GOLD	PURVIS	CHARLESTON	HOPE
HAMMOCK	BLOCKADE	CRADLE	PRESSED	CANDLES

Slave Dancer

SHROUDS	AFRICA	REVENUE	CREOLE	COCKROACH
MACAROON	IBOS	BOLLWEEVIL	BEN	SLAVE
SHARKS	BENIN	FREE SPACE	JESSIE	MOONLIGHT
THIRTEEN	FIFE	CAWTHORNE	CASKS	RAFT
GALLEY	APPRENTICE	STAR	SPARK	RAS

Slave Dancer

PURVIS	SPARK	RAS	MOONLIGHT	NED
CRADLE	RAFT	SLAVE	HOPE	COCKROACH
GALLEY	AFRICA	FREE SPACE	DANIEL	GOLD
CAWTHORNE	STAR	CHARLESTON	BEAULIEU	NEEDLE
REVENUE	LIME	CONGO	PRESSED	JESSIE

Slave Dancer

MACAROON	CURRY	AGATHA	CANDLES	BENIN
BOLLWEEVIL	BETTY	CUBA	CASKS	IBOS
LOUT	CREOLE	FREE SPACE	CARRE	SHROUDS
THIRTEEN	FLYING	SHARKS	BEN	BOOM
CHICKEN	HAMMOCK	SWIM	PRIVATEERS	APPRENTICE

Slave Dancer

BOOM	BLOCKADE	CREOLE	COCKROACH	MOONLIGHT
SHROUDS	GALLEY	NED	CURRY	BENIN
SLAVE	SWIM	FREE SPACE	PRESSED	FIFE
NEEDLE	RAFT	LIME	CASKS	SPARK
HAMMOCK	CHARLESTON	AFRICA	BEN	SHARKS

Slave Dancer

RAS	BEAULIEU	PRIVATEERS	HOPE	IBOS
CUBA	STAR	APPRENTICE	JESSIE	CANDLES
BETTY	DANIEL	FREE SPACE	CARRE	REVENUE
CHICKEN	BOLLWEEVIL	CONGO	LOUT	PURVIS
AGATHA	MACAROON	CAWTHORNE	THIRTEEN	CRADLE

Slave Dancer

NEEDLE	LOUT	NED	REVENUE	BOOM
BLOCKADE	CURRY	PRIVATEERS	COCKROACH	RAFT
AFRICA	SPARK	FREE SPACE	CUBA	BOLLWEEVIL
CHICKEN	RAS	MOONLIGHT	MACAROON	GOLD
THIRTEEN	GALLEY	PRESSED	FLYING	FIFE

Slave Dancer

CHARLESTON	LIME	CANDLES	SWIM	STAR
CREOLE	JESSIE	PURVIS	CASKS	BENIN
AGATHA	HAMMOCK	FREE SPACE	BEAULIEU	IBOS
CAWTHORNE	BEN	SHROUDS	APPRENTICE	SLAVE
CRADLE	SHARKS	HOPE	CARRE	CONGO

Slave Dancer

LIME	BEN	PURVIS	IBOS	HAMMOCK
REVENUE	CANDLES	MACAROON	CRADLE	CONGO
AGATHA	CASKS	FREE SPACE	AFRICA	NED
NEEDLE	SWIM	PRESSED	APPRENTICE	SHROUDS
COCKROACH	THIRTEEN	CURRY	DANIEL	BLOCKADE

Slave Dancer

CAWTHORNE	RAFT	SLAVE	FIFE	PRIVATEERS
BENIN	BETTY	GOLD	BEAULIEU	BOOM
HOPE	LOUT	FREE SPACE	CHICKEN	SHARKS
GALLEY	CHARLESTON	SPARK	CARRE	JESSIE
CREOLE	STAR	FLYING	CUBA	MOONLIGHT

Slave Dancer

SHARKS	FIFE	CREOLE	APPRENTICE	BENIN
HOPE	CANDLES	CARRE	RAFT	SLAVE
DANIEL	CASKS	FREE SPACE	LIME	CRADLE
BOOM	THIRTEEN	SWIM	AFRICA	BETTY
CURRY	CAWTHORNE	PURVIS	GOLD	MACAROON

Slave Dancer

BEAULIEU	MOONLIGHT	SPARK	JESSIE	LOUT
AGATHA	HAMMOCK	COCKROACH	NEEDLE	CONGO
CHICKEN	RAS	FREE SPACE	NED	REVENUE
CHARLESTON	PRIVATEERS	CUBA	GALLEY	BOLLWEEVIL
PRESSED	BEN	SHROUDS	BLOCKADE	STAR

Slave Dancer

MACAROON	RAFT	SPARK	AGATHA	DANIEL
BETTY	PRIVATEERS	LOUT	PURVIS	IBOS
MOONLIGHT	SHARKS	FREE SPACE	JESSIE	RAS
BEN	CHICKEN	CASKS	CAWTHORNE	REVENUE
GALLEY	CURRY	PRESSED	BOLLWEEVIL	GOLD

Slave Dancer

NEEDLE	NED	FIFE	SLAVE	SHROUDS
CONGO	FLYING	HAMMOCK	CHARLESTON	CREOLE
APPRENTICE	SWIM	FREE SPACE	BEAULIEU	BOOM
COCKROACH	HOPE	STAR	CARRE	CANDLES
LIME	THIRTEEN	AFRICA	BENIN	BLOCKADE

Slave Dancer

LIME	REVENUE	SWIM	SHROUDS	CRADLE
BLOCKADE	CANDLES	RAFT	CONGO	CUBA
HOPE	CARRE	FREE SPACE	THIRTEEN	AGATHA
JESSIE	PURVIS	GOLD	DANIEL	BEAULIEU
APPRENTICE	SLAVE	GALLEY	SPARK	NED

Slave Dancer

CHICKEN	MOONLIGHT	PRIVATEERS	BENIN	BEN
LOUT	AFRICA	STAR	RAS	CURRY
FIFE	CAWTHORNE	FREE SPACE	HAMMOCK	PRESSED
CASKS	CREOLE	COCKROACH	BOOM	FLYING
CHARLESTON	BOLLWEEVIL	NEEDLE	MACAROON	IBOS

Slave Dancer

BOLLWEEVIL	THIRTEEN	SWIM	REVENUE	GALLEY
SHARKS	HAMMOCK	BEN	PRESSED	RAS
BOOM	BETTY	FREE SPACE	HOPE	CHICKEN
CAWTHORNE	NED	CONGO	NEEDLE	COCKROACH
SLAVE	IBOS	PURVIS	CARRE	LOUT

Slave Dancer

MACAROON	APPRENTICE	BLOCKADE	CUBA	BENIN
CREOLE	RAFT	MOONLIGHT	CURRY	CHARLESTON
LIME	BEAULIEU	FREE SPACE	SPARK	CRADLE
AGATHA	SHROUDS	STAR	GOLD	AFRICA
CANDLES	FLYING	FIFE	CASKS	JESSIE

Slave Dancer

FLYING	FIFE	RAS	CARRE	AGATHA
CAWTHORNE	SWIM	CUBA	PURVIS	COCKROACH
MOONLIGHT	BLOCKADE	FREE SPACE	RAFT	AFRICA
LIME	LOUT	CASKS	CREOLE	NEEDLE
CHICKEN	BENIN	SHROUDS	BOLLWEEVIL	NED

Slave Dancer

CHARLESTON	PRIVATEERS	PRESSED	CANDLES	REVENUE
APPRENTICE	SPARK	HAMMOCK	IBOS	SHARKS
BETTY	DANIEL	FREE SPACE	BEAULIEU	JESSIE
BEN	GALLEY	CRADLE	SLAVE	MACAROON
THIRTEEN	BOOM	HOPE	STAR	CONGO

Slave Dancer

HOPE	BEN	BENIN	JESSIE	COCKROACH
CHICKEN	SHROUDS	CUBA	CHARLESTON	SWIM
GOLD	SPARK	FREE SPACE	AFRICA	AGATHA
BLOCKADE	MACAROON	NEEDLE	BOOM	PURVIS
BOLLWEEVIL	PRIVATEERS	STAR	BETTY	RAFT

Slave Dancer

CAWTHORNE	PRESSED	HAMMOCK	CURRY	NED
MOONLIGHT	APPRENTICE	THIRTEEN	CARRE	CREOLE
CASKS	CONGO	FREE SPACE	SLAVE	LIME
RAS	DANIEL	GALLEY	CANDLES	FLYING
LOUT	FIFE	REVENUE	CRADLE	BEAULIEU

Slave Dancer

PRESSED	STAR	CARRE	CONGO	GALLEY
CASKS	LOUT	APPRENTICE	IBOS	CREOLE
AGATHA	NEEDLE	FREE SPACE	DANIEL	NED
BENIN	SPARK	HAMMOCK	LIME	COCKROACH
MOONLIGHT	FLYING	CUBA	PURVIS	THIRTEEN

Slave Dancer

CHICKEN	AFRICA	BOLLWEEVIL	SWIM	FIFE
BOOM	SHROUDS	CAWTHORNE	SHARKS	GOLD
BEN	PRIVATEERS	FREE SPACE	BETTY	CHARLESTON
BLOCKADE	MACAROON	CANDLES	CURRY	CRADLE
REVENUE	JESSIE	RAS	BEAULIEU	RAFT

Slave Dancer

SHARKS	NEEDLE	LOUT	IBOS	CHICKEN
FLYING	MACAROON	MOONLIGHT	RAS	CONGO
DANIEL	THIRTEEN	FREE SPACE	STAR	GALLEY
BENIN	SLAVE	BEN	CARRE	PRIVATEERS
RAFT	CAWTHORNE	CREOLE	GOLD	NED

Slave Dancer

BLOCKADE	SPARK	CURRY	PURVIS	BEAULIEU
PRESSED	CANDLES	CASKS	SWIM	CUBA
APPRENTICE	REVENUE	FREE SPACE	FIFE	AGATHA
AFRICA	BETTY	COCKROACH	SHROUDS	BOOM
BOLLWEEVIL	CRADLE	JESSIE	LIME	HAMMOCK

Slave Dancer

APPRENTICE	GOLD	PRESSED	CANDLES	BENIN
AFRICA	RAFT	RAS	COCKROACH	AGATHA
BOOM	IBOS	FREE SPACE	BLOCKADE	CHARLESTON
HOPE	MOONLIGHT	BEN	CREOLE	DANIEL
LOUT	CARRE	NEEDLE	REVENUE	BETTY

Slave Dancer

SHROUDS	STAR	GALLEY	SWIM	NED
CRADLE	SPARK	CASKS	JESSIE	PURVIS
CHICKEN	PRIVATEERS	FREE SPACE	CAWTHORNE	THIRTEEN
FIFE	CONGO	LIME	BEAULIEU	CUBA
CURRY	SHARKS	FLYING	SLAVE	MACAROON

Slave Dancer

APPRENTICE	BEAULIEU	MACAROON	CANDLES	PRESSED
BOLLWEEVIL	PURVIS	PRIVATEERS	LOUT	SPARK
SHROUDS	IBOS	FREE SPACE	SLAVE	CHICKEN
CREOLE	CASKS	NED	LIME	SWIM
CARRE	FIFE	BLOCKADE	MOONLIGHT	SHARKS

Slave Dancer

CONGO	REVENUE	GOLD	BETTY	BENIN
THIRTEEN	AFRICA	CRADLE	RAS	BEN
CHARLESTON	BOOM	FREE SPACE	AGATHA	STAR
HAMMOCK	CURRY	CAWTHORNE	FLYING	COCKROACH
JESSIE	NEEDLE	HOPE	RAFT	CUBA

Slave Dancer Vocabulary Word List

No.	Word	Clue/Definition
1.	ADDLES	Confuses
2.	AFFLICTION	Disease
3.	AGGRIEVED	Pained
4.	ALOOFNESS	Indifference
5.	AMIABLY	Pleasantly
6.	APOTHECARY	Druggist; pharmacist
7.	ARMAMENT	Arms; weapons
8.	ASSUAGE	Ease; relieve
9.	ATHWART	Crosswise; at right angles with the ship's keel
10.	BARBAROUSNESS	Horribly cruel
11.	BARRACOON	Enclosure of slaves
12.	BEGRIMED	Grimy; filthy
13.	BRINY	Salty sea water
14.	BROCADE	Surly
15.	CABOCIERO	Portuguese slave broker
16.	CAPTIOUS	Faultfinding
17.	CARRONADE	Small cannon
18.	CHAGRINED	Annoyed
19.	CHANDLER	Candle and supplies merchant
20.	CHAOS	Confusion; disorder
21.	CLAMOR	Uproar
22.	CONFOUNDING	Puzzling; flustering
23.	CONVULSION	Contraction; shaking
24.	CULPRIT	Guilty party
25.	DEBASED	Dishonorable
26.	DECAPITATION	Beheading
27.	DEFIED	Boldly resisted
28.	DEFILE	Gully; ravine
29.	DEMENTED	Crazy; mad
30.	DEPRAVED	Corrupted
31.	DOLDRUMS	Region of calm winds near the equator
32.	ENVISAGE	Picture
33.	FESTIVITY	Celebration
34.	FETID	Foul
35.	FLOGGED	Lashed; whipped
36.	HARROWING	Frightening
37.	HOLYSTONED	Scrubbed clean by a soft sandstone
38.	IMPALED	Fenced in
39.	IMPASSIVELY	Without expression
40.	IMPENETRABLE	Dense; thick
41.	IMPERTINENT	Sassy; fresh
42.	INDISTINCT	Unclear
43.	INGENIOUS	Brilliant
44.	JETTISON	Abandon; get rid of
45.	KEENING	Wailing; mourning
46.	LAMENT	Wail; sob
47.	LANGUOROUS	Sleepy; lazy
48.	LOFTY	Noble
49.	LUCRATIVE	Profitable
50.	LUDICROUS	Ridiculous
51.	LUMINOUS	Glowing radiant
52.	MARTIAL	Military; warlike
53.	MELANCHOLY	Mournful

Slave Dancer Vocabulary Word List

No.	Word	Clue/Definition
54.	MIMICKED	Imitated
55.	MORTAL	Deadly; fatal
56.	MORTIFIED	Shamed; embarrassed
57.	MUTINIES	Revolts; uprisings
58.	OBSCURE	Unknown; unfamiliar
59.	PENETRATE	Enter; come through
60.	PENSIVELY	Thoughtfully
61.	PERILOUS	Dangerous
62.	PERPLEXED	Puzzled
63.	PLACIDLY	Peacefully
64.	PLIGHT	Sorry situation
65.	PLUMB	Absolute; exact
66.	PRESSGANGED	Forced onto ship service
67.	PROFUSION	Excess
68.	PROTESTATIONS	Objections
69.	RANCID	Rotten; foul
70.	RECUMBENT	Leaning; idle
71.	REFLECTIVELY	Deliberately; with meaning
72.	RELINQUISH	Give up
73.	RESTRAINT	Control; restriction
74.	REVIVIFIED	Rekindled; revived
75.	SENTINEL	Guard
76.	SHAMBLING	Shuffling
77.	SPRY	Limber; agile
78.	SUSTAINED	Supported
79.	TRANQUIL	Peaceful
80.	TRUSSED	Tied up
81.	TURBULENT	Roaring; blustery
82.	UNCHARITABLE	Hard hearted
83.	UNDETERRED	Unstopped
84.	UNDIGNIFIED	Tasteless
85.	VILE	Foul
86.	WHEEDLING	Charming or coaxing; flattering
87.	WRACK	Seaweed

Slave Dancer Vocabulary Fill In The Blank 1

_____   1. Pleasantly

_____   2. Imitated

_____   3. Horribly cruel

_____   4. Glowing radiant

_____   5. Forced onto ship service

_____   6. Deadly; fatal

_____   7. Guilty party

_____   8. Guard

_____   9. Fenced in

_____   10. Roaring; blustery

_____   11. Confusion; disorder

_____   12. Druggist; pharmacist

_____   13. Shamed; embarrassed

_____   14. Salty sea water

_____   15. Wailing; mourning

_____   16. Contraction; shaking

_____   17. Without expression

_____   18. Rotten; foul

_____   19. Peacefully

_____   20. Pained

Slave Dancer Vocabulary Fill In The Blank 1 Answer Key

AMIABLY	1. Pleasantly
MIMICKED	2. Imitated
BARBAROUSNESS	3. Horribly cruel
LUMINOUS	4. Glowing radiant
PRESSGANGED	5. Forced onto ship service
MORTAL	6. Deadly; fatal
CULPRIT	7. Guilty party
SENTINEL	8. Guard
IMPALED	9. Fenced in
TURBULENT	10. Roaring; blustery
CHAOS	11. Confusion; disorder
APOTHECARY	12. Druggist; pharmacist
MORTIFIED	13. Shamed; embarrassed
BRINY	14. Salty sea water
KEENING	15. Wailing; mourning
CONVULSION	16. Contraction; shaking
IMPASSIVELY	17. Without expression
RANCID	18. Rotten; foul
PLACIDLY	19. Peacefully
AGGRIEVED	20. Pained

Slave Dancer Vocabulary Fill In The Blank 2

_____ 1. Unknown; unfamiliar

_____ 2. Mournful

_____ 3. Dishonorable

_____ 4. Tied up

_____ 5. Hard hearted

_____ 6. Ridiculous

_____ 7. Deadly; fatal

_____ 8. Leaning; idle

_____ 9. Supported

_____ 10. Candle and supplies merchant

_____ 11. Sassy; fresh

_____ 12. Unstopped

_____ 13. Sleepy; lazy

_____ 14. Objections

_____ 15. Crazy; mad

_____ 16. Boldly resisted

_____ 17. Give up

_____ 18. Pleasantly

_____ 19. Arms; weapons

_____ 20. Shamed; embarrassed

Slave Dancer Vocabulary Fill In The Blank 2 Answer Key

OBSCURE	1.	Unknown; unfamiliar
MELANCHOLY	2.	Mournful
DEBASED	3.	Dishonorable
TRUSSED	4.	Tied up
UNCHARITABLE	5.	Hard hearted
LUDICROUS	6.	Ridiculous
MORTAL	7.	Deadly; fatal
RECUMBENT	8.	Leaning; idle
SUSTAINED	9.	Supported
CHANDLER	10.	Candle and supplies merchant
IMPERTINENT	11.	Sassy; fresh
UNDETERRED	12.	Unstopped
LANGUOROUS	13.	Sleepy; lazy
PROTESTATIONS	14.	Objections
DEMENTED	15.	Crazy; mad
DEFIED	16.	Boldly resisted
RELINQUISH	17.	Give up
AMIABLY	18.	Pleasantly
ARMAMENT	19.	Arms; weapons
MORTIFIED	20.	Shamed; embarrassed

Slave Dancer Vocabulary Fill In The Blank 3

_____ 1. Seaweed

_____ 2. Druggist; pharmacist

_____ 3. Puzzled

_____ 4. Revolts; uprisings

_____ 5. Lashed; whipped

_____ 6. Ridiculous

_____ 7. Disease

_____ 8. Sorry situation

_____ 9. Brilliant

_____ 10. Guard

_____ 11. Dishonorable

_____ 12. Peaceful

_____ 13. Wail; sob

_____ 14. Mournful

_____ 15. Guilty party

_____ 16. Frightening

_____ 17. Deliberately; with meaning

_____ 18. Grimy; filthy

_____ 19. Unknown; unfamiliar

_____ 20. Shuffling

Slave Dancer Vocabulary Fill In The Blank 3 Answer Key

WRACK	1. Seaweed
APOTHECARY	2. Druggist; pharmacist
PERPLEXED	3. Puzzled
MUTINIES	4. Revolts; uprisings
FLOGGED	5. Lashed; whipped
LUDICROUS	6. Ridiculous
AFFLICTION	7. Disease
PLIGHT	8. Sorry situation
INGENIOUS	9. Brilliant
SENTINEL	10. Guard
DEBASED	11. Dishonorable
TRANQUIL	12. Peaceful
LAMENT	13. Wail; sob
MELANCHOLY	14. Mournful
CULPRIT	15. Guilty party
HARROWING	16. Frightening
REFLECTIVELY	17. Deliberately; with meaning
BEGRIMED	18. Grimy; filthy
OBSCURE	19. Unknown; unfamiliar
SHAMBLING	20. Shuffling

Slave Dancer Vocabulary Fill In The Blank 4

_____ 1. Fenced in

_____ 2. Forced onto ship service

_____ 3. Glowing radiant

_____ 4. Enclosure of slaves

_____ 5. Control; restriction

_____ 6. Contraction; shaking

_____ 7. Imitated

_____ 8. Disease

_____ 9. Noble

_____ 10. Guilty party

_____ 11. Faultfinding

_____ 12. Frightening

_____ 13. Unknown; unfamiliar

_____ 14. Abandon; get rid of

_____ 15. Enter; come through

_____ 16. Thoughtfully

_____ 17. Ridiculous

_____ 18. Without expression

_____ 19. Give up

_____ 20. Salty sea water

Slave Dancer Vocabulary Fill In The Blank 4 Answer Key

IMPALED	1. Fenced in
PRESSGANGED	2. Forced onto ship service
LUMINOUS	3. Glowing radiant
BARRACOON	4. Enclosure of slaves
RESTRAINT	5. Control; restriction
CONVULSION	6. Contraction; shaking
MIMICKED	7. Imitated
AFFLICTION	8. Disease
LOFTY	9. Noble
CULPRIT	10. Guilty party
CAPTIOUS	11. Faultfinding
HARROWING	12. Frightening
OBSCURE	13. Unknown; unfamiliar
JETTISON	14. Abandon; get rid of
PENETRATE	15. Enter; come through
PENSIVELY	16. Thoughtfully
LUDICROUS	17. Ridiculous
IMPASSIVELY	18. Without expression
RELINQUISH	19. Give up
BRINY	20. Salty sea water

Slave Dancer Vocabulary Matching 1

___ 1. CHAOS   A. Druggist; pharmacist
___ 2. FETID   B. Enter; come through
___ 3. RECUMBENT   C. Picture
___ 4. UNCHARITABLE   D. Uproar
___ 5. VILE   E. Hard hearted
___ 6. AFFLICTION   F. Boldly resisted
___ 7. DEFILE   G. Control; restriction
___ 8. ENVISAGE   H. Disease
___ 9. BARBAROUSNESS I. Gully; ravine
___10. PENSIVELY   J. Sassy; fresh
___11. DEFIED   K. Thoughtfully
___12. REFLECTIVELY   L. Leaning; idle
___13. CLAMOR   M. Charming or coaxing; flattering
___14. TRUSSED   N. Profitable
___15. DEMENTED   O. Foul
___16. PLIGHT   P. Ease; relieve
___17. LUCRATIVE   Q. Crazy; mad
___18. APOTHECARY   R. Tied up
___19. MORTIFIED   S. Confusion; disorder
___20. ASSUAGE   T. Horribly cruel
___21. FLOGGED   U. Lashed; whipped
___22. IMPERTINENT   V. Foul
___23. PENETRATE   W. Shamed; embarrassed
___24. RESTRAINT   X. Deliberately; with meaning
___25. WHEEDLING   Y. Sorry situation

Slave Dancer Vocabulary Matching 1 Answer Key

S - 1. CHAOS	A.	Druggist; pharmacist
V - 2. FETID	B.	Enter; come through
L - 3. RECUMBENT	C.	Picture
E - 4. UNCHARITABLE	D.	Uproar
O - 5. VILE	E.	Hard hearted
H - 6. AFFLICTION	F.	Boldly resisted
I - 7. DEFILE	G.	Control; restriction
C - 8. ENVISAGE	H.	Disease
T - 9. BARBAROUSNESS	I.	Gully; ravine
K - 10. PENSIVELY	J.	Sassy; fresh
F - 11. DEFIED	K.	Thoughtfully
X - 12. REFLECTIVELY	L.	Leaning; idle
D - 13. CLAMOR	M.	Charming or coaxing; flattering
R - 14. TRUSSED	N.	Profitable
Q - 15. DEMENTED	O.	Foul
Y - 16. PLIGHT	P.	Ease; relieve
N - 17. LUCRATIVE	Q.	Crazy; mad
A - 18. APOTHECARY	R.	Tied up
W - 19. MORTIFIED	S.	Confusion; disorder
P - 20. ASSUAGE	T.	Horribly cruel
U - 21. FLOGGED	U.	Lashed; whipped
J - 22. IMPERTINENT	V.	Foul
B - 23. PENETRATE	W.	Shamed; embarrassed
G - 24. RESTRAINT	X.	Deliberately; with meaning
M - 25. WHEEDLING	Y.	Sorry situation

Slave Dancer Vocabulary Matching 2

___ 1. ATHWART   A. Deadly; fatal
___ 2. FESTIVITY   B. Charming or coaxing; flattering
___ 3. CHANDLER   C. Wail; sob
___ 4. DEPRAVED   D. Crosswise; at right angles with the ship's keel
___ 5. MORTAL   E. Corrupted
___ 6. MIMICKED   F. Pleasantly
___ 7. WHEEDLING   G. Revolts; uprisings
___ 8. AMIABLY   H. Picture
___ 9. REFLECTIVELY   I. Celebration
___10. ADDLES   J. Hard hearted
___11. CABOCIERO   K. Deliberately; with meaning
___12. MUTINIES   L. Lashed; whipped
___13. FLOGGED   M. Enter; come through
___14. IMPERTINENT   N. Scrubbed clean by a soft sandstone
___15. HOLYSTONED   O. Portuguese slave broker
___16. DEBASED   P. Confuses
___17. PENETRATE   Q. Sassy; fresh
___18. CARRONADE   R. Candle and supplies merchant
___19. VILE   S. Imitated
___20. LAMENT   T. Control; restriction
___21. ENVISAGE   U. Foul
___22. RESTRAINT   V. Dishonorable
___23. LOFTY   W. Noble
___24. LANGUOROUS   X. Sleepy; lazy
___25. UNCHARITABLE   Y. Small cannon

Slave Dancer Vocabulary Matching 2 Answer Key

D - 1. ATHWART	A.	Deadly; fatal
I - 2. FESTIVITY	B.	Charming or coaxing; flattering
R - 3. CHANDLER	C.	Wail; sob
E - 4. DEPRAVED	D.	Crosswise; at right angles with the ship's keel
A - 5. MORTAL	E.	Corrupted
S - 6. MIMICKED	F.	Pleasantly
B - 7. WHEEDLING	G.	Revolts; uprisings
F - 8. AMIABLY	H.	Picture
K - 9. REFLECTIVELY	I.	Celebration
P - 10. ADDLES	J.	Hard hearted
O - 11. CABOCIERO	K.	Deliberately; with meaning
G - 12. MUTINIES	L.	Lashed; whipped
L - 13. FLOGGED	M.	Enter; come through
Q - 14. IMPERTINENT	N.	Scrubbed clean by a soft sandstone
N - 15. HOLYSTONED	O.	Portuguese slave broker
V - 16. DEBASED	P.	Confuses
M - 17. PENETRATE	Q.	Sassy; fresh
Y - 18. CARRONADE	R.	Candle and supplies merchant
U - 19. VILE	S.	Imitated
C - 20. LAMENT	T.	Control; restriction
H - 21. ENVISAGE	U.	Foul
T - 22. RESTRAINT	V.	Dishonorable
W - 23. LOFTY	W.	Noble
X - 24. LANGUOROUS	X.	Sleepy; lazy
J - 25. UNCHARITABLE	Y.	Small cannon

Slave Dancer Vocabulary Matching 3

___ 1. RELINQUISH   A. Crazy; mad
___ 2. JETTISON   B. Limber; agile
___ 3. MORTIFIED   C. Celebration
___ 4. IMPALED   D. Absolute; exact
___ 5. CLAMOR   E. Excess
___ 6. CHANDLER   F. Peacefully
___ 7. PLUMB   G. Forced onto ship service
___ 8. DOLDRUMS   H. Fenced in
___ 9. HARROWING   I. Profitable
___10. TURBULENT   J. Abandon; get rid of
___11. PENETRATE   K. Enter; come through
___12. SPRY   L. Leaning; idle
___13. PLACIDLY   M. Give up
___14. PENSIVELY   N. Thoughtfully
___15. PROFUSION   O. Shamed; embarrassed
___16. LUCRATIVE   P. Annoyed
___17. PRESSGANGED   Q. Frightening
___18. CHAGRINED   R. Region of calm winds near the equator
___19. RECUMBENT   S. Uproar
___20. MARTIAL   T. Candle and supplies merchant
___21. DEMENTED   U. Brilliant
___22. SHAMBLING   V. Military; warlike
___23. RANCID   W. Roaring; blustery
___24. INGENIOUS   X. Rotten; foul
___25. FESTIVITY   Y. Shuffling

Slave Dancer Vocabulary Matching 3 Answer Key

M - 1.	RELINQUISH	A.	Crazy; mad
J - 2.	JETTISON	B.	Limber; agile
O - 3.	MORTIFIED	C.	Celebration
H - 4.	IMPALED	D.	Absolute; exact
S - 5.	CLAMOR	E.	Excess
T - 6.	CHANDLER	F.	Peacefully
D - 7.	PLUMB	G.	Forced onto ship service
R - 8.	DOLDRUMS	H.	Fenced in
Q - 9.	HARROWING	I.	Profitable
W - 10.	TURBULENT	J.	Abandon; get rid of
K - 11.	PENETRATE	K.	Enter; come through
B - 12.	SPRY	L.	Leaning; idle
F - 13.	PLACIDLY	M.	Give up
N - 14.	PENSIVELY	N.	Thoughtfully
E - 15.	PROFUSION	O.	Shamed; embarrassed
I - 16.	LUCRATIVE	P.	Annoyed
G - 17.	PRESSGANGED	Q.	Frightening
P - 18.	CHAGRINED	R.	Region of calm winds near the equator
L - 19.	RECUMBENT	S.	Uproar
V - 20.	MARTIAL	T.	Candle and supplies merchant
A - 21.	DEMENTED	U.	Brilliant
Y - 22.	SHAMBLING	V.	Military; warlike
X - 23.	RANCID	W.	Roaring; blustery
U - 24.	INGENIOUS	X.	Rotten; foul
C - 25.	FESTIVITY	Y.	Shuffling

Slave Dancer Vocabulary Matching 4

___ 1. WRACK   A. Imitated
___ 2. REFLECTIVELY   B. Deliberately; with meaning
___ 3. LUMINOUS   C. Confusion; disorder
___ 4. CHAOS   D. Disease
___ 5. LUCRATIVE   E. Seaweed
___ 6. SUSTAINED   F. Beheading
___ 7. MIMICKED   G. Dense; thick
___ 8. AFFLICTION   H. Abandon; get rid of
___ 9. JETTISON   I. Indifference
___ 10. PENETRATE   J. Glowing radiant
___ 11. MARTIAL   K. Pained
___ 12. AGGRIEVED   L. Ease; relieve
___ 13. CABOCIERO   M. Leaning; idle
___ 14. LANGOROUS   N. Noble
___ 15. IMPASSIVELY   O. Horribly cruel
___ 16. ASSUAGE   P. Guard
___ 17. BARBAROUSNESS   Q. Military; warlike
___ 18. DECAPITATION   R. Enter; come through
___ 19. LOFTY   S. Brilliant
___ 20. INGENIOUS   T. Profitable
___ 21. RECUMBENT   U. Sleepy; lazy
___ 22. CONFOUNDING   V. Supported
___ 23. SENTINEL   W. Puzzling; flustering
___ 24. ALOOFNESS   X. Portuguese slave broker
___ 25. IMPENETRABLE   Y. Without expression

Slave Dancer Vocabulary Matching 4 Answer Key

E - 1. WRACK		A. Imitated
B - 2. REFLECTIVELY		B. Deliberately; with meaning
J - 3. LUMINOUS		C. Confusion; disorder
C - 4. CHAOS		D. Disease
T - 5. LUCRATIVE		E. Seaweed
V - 6. SUSTAINED		F. Beheading
A - 7. MIMICKED		G. Dense; thick
D - 8. AFFLICTION		H. Abandon; get rid of
H - 9. JETTISON		I. Indifference
R - 10. PENETRATE		J. Glowing radiant
Q - 11. MARTIAL		K. Pained
K - 12. AGGRIEVED		L. Ease; relieve
X - 13. CABOCIERO		M. Leaning; idle
U - 14. LANGOROUS		N. Noble
Y - 15. IMPASSIVELY		O. Horribly cruel
L - 16. ASSUAGE		P. Guard
O - 17. BARBAROUSNESS		Q. Military; warlike
F - 18. DECAPITATION		R. Enter; come through
N - 19. LOFTY		S. Brilliant
S - 20. INGENIOUS		T. Profitable
M - 21. RECUMBENT		U. Sleepy; lazy
W - 22. CONFOUNDING		V. Supported
P - 23. SENTINEL		W. Puzzling; flustering
I - 24. ALOOFNESS		X. Portuguese slave broker
G - 25. IMPENETRABLE		Y. Without expression

Slave Dancer Vocabulary Magic Squares 1

Match the definition with the vocabulary word. Put your answers in the magic squares below. When your answers are correct, all columns and rows will add to the same number.

A. BARBAROUSNESS
B. DEPRAVED
C. MIMICKED
D. DOLDRUMS
E. ARMAMENT
F. JETTISON
G. VILE
H. HOLYSTONED
I. CAPTIOUS
J. WHEEDLING
K. INDISTINCT
L. TURBULENT
M. LUDICROUS
N. CLAMOR
O. AMIABLY
P. RECUMBENT

1. Pleasantly
2. Charming or coaxing; flattering
3. Scrubbed clean by a soft sandstone
4. Horribly cruel
5. Region of calm winds near the equator
6. Arms; weapons
7. Unclear
8. Uproar
9. Abandon; get rid of
10. Imitated
11. Ridiculous
12. Roaring; blustery
13. Faultfinding
14. Leaning; idle
15. Corrupted
16. Foul

A=	B=	C=	D=
E=	F=	G=	H=
I=	J=	K=	L=
M=	N=	O=	P=

Slave Dancer Vocabulary Magic Squares 1 Answer Key

Match the definition with the vocabulary word. Put your answers in the magic squares below. When your answers are correct, all columns and rows will add to the same number.

A. BARBAROUSNESS
B. DEPRAVED
C. MIMICKED
D. DOLDRUMS
E. ARMAMENT
F. JETTISON
G. VILE
H. HOLYSTONED
I. CAPTIOUS
J. WHEEDLING
K. INDISTINCT
L. TURBULENT
M. LUDICROUS
N. CLAMOR
O. AMIABLY
P. RECUMBENT

1. Pleasantly
2. Charming or coaxing; flattering
3. Scrubbed clean by a soft sandstone
4. Horribly cruel
5. Region of calm winds near the equator
6. Arms; weapons
7. Unclear
8. Uproar
9. Abandon; get rid of
10. Imitated
11. Ridiculous
12. Roaring; blustery
13. Faultfinding
14. Leaning; idle
15. Corrupted
16. Foul

A=4	B=15	C=10	D=5
E=6	F=9	G=16	H=3
I=13	J=2	K=7	L=12
M=11	N=8	O=1	P=14

Slave Dancer Vocabulary Magic Squares 2

Match the definition with the vocabulary word. Put your answers in the magic squares below. When your answers are correct, all columns and rows will add to the same number.

A. RELINQUISH
B. PLIGHT
C. PROTESTATIONS
D. FLOGGED
E. PERPLEXED
F. PENETRATE
G. IMPERTINENT
H. CHAGRINED
I. RESTRAINT
J. MIMICKED
K. APOTHECARY
L. DEFIED
M. FESTIVITY
N. TURBULENT
O. WHEEDLING
P. ASSUAGE

1. Enter; come through
2. Control; restriction
3. Charming or coaxing; flattering
4. Lashed; whipped
5. Celebration
6. Sorry situation
7. Annoyed
8. Druggist; pharmacist
9. Objections
10. Ease; relieve
11. Imitated
12. Puzzled
13. Boldly resisted
14. Sassy; fresh
15. Give up
16. Roaring; blustery

A=	B=	C=	D=
E=	F=	G=	H=
I=	J=	K=	L=
M=	N=	O=	P=

Slave Dancer Vocabulary Magic Squares 2 Answer Key

Match the definition with the vocabulary word. Put your answers in the magic squares below. When your answers are correct, all columns and rows will add to the same number.

A. RELINQUISH
B. PLIGHT
C. PROTESTATIONS
D. FLOGGED
E. PERPLEXED
F. PENETRATE
G. IMPERTINENT
H. CHAGRINED
I. RESTRAINT
J. MIMICKED
K. APOTHECARY
L. DEFIED
M. FESTIVITY
N. TURBULENT
O. WHEEDLING
P. ASSUAGE

1. Enter; come through
2. Control; restriction
3. Charming or coaxing; flattering
4. Lashed; whipped
5. Celebration
6. Sorry situation
7. Annoyed
8. Druggist; pharmacist
9. Objections
10. Ease; relieve
11. Imitated
12. Puzzled
13. Boldly resisted
14. Sassy; fresh
15. Give up
16. Roaring; blustery

A=15	B=6	C=9	D=4
E=12	F=1	G=14	H=7
I=2	J=11	K=8	L=13
M=5	N=16	O=3	P=10

Slave Dancer Vocabulary Magic Squares 3

Match the definition with the vocabulary word. Put your answers in the magic squares below. When your answers are correct, all columns and rows will add to the same number.

A. CHAGRINED
B. PROFUSION
C. LUMINOUS
D. OBSCURE
E. MELANCHOLY
F. DECAPITATION
G. HARROWING
H. TRUSSED
I. AMIABLY
J. DEBASED
K. ARMAMENT
L. VILE
M. PENSIVELY
N. INGENIOUS
O. PROTESTATIONS
P. BARRACOON

1. Annoyed
2. Brilliant
3. Dishonorable
4. Mournful
5. Frightening
6. Foul
7. Enclosure of slaves
8. Glowing radiant
9. Objections
10. Unknown; unfamiliar
11. Tied up
12. Arms; weapons
13. Pleasantly
14. Beheading
15. Excess
16. Thoughtfully

A=	B=	C=	D=
E=	F=	G=	H=
I=	J=	K=	L=
M=	N=	O=	P=

Slave Dancer Vocabulary Magic Squares 3 Answer Key

Match the definition with the vocabulary word. Put your answers in the magic squares below. When your answers are correct, all columns and rows will add to the same number.

A. CHAGRINED
B. PROFUSION
C. LUMINOUS
D. OBSCURE
E. MELANCHOLY
F. DECAPITATION
G. HARROWING
H. TRUSSED
I. AMIABLY
J. DEBASED
K. ARMAMENT
L. VILE
M. PENSIVELY
N. INGENIOUS
O. PROTESTATIONS
P. BARRACOON

1. Annoyed
2. Brilliant
3. Dishonorable
4. Mournful
5. Frightening
6. Foul
7. Enclosure of slaves
8. Glowing radiant
9. Objections
10. Unknown; unfamiliar
11. Tied up
12. Arms; weapons
13. Pleasantly
14. Beheading
15. Excess
16. Thoughtfully

A=1	B=15	C=8	D=10
E=4	F=14	G=5	H=11
I=13	J=3	K=12	L=6
M=16	N=2	O=9	P=7

Slave Dancer Vocabulary Magic Squares 4

Match the definition with the vocabulary word. Put your answers in the magic squares below. When your answers are correct, all columns and rows will add to the same number.

A. APOTHECARY
B. RESTRAINT
C. MORTIFIED
D. MELANCHOLY
E. INGENIOUS
F. CULPRIT
G. PENETRATE
H. SENTINEL
I. TRANQUIL
J. AFFLICTION
K. CHAGRINED
L. RANCID
M. BROCADE
N. LOFTY
O. KEENING
P. CARRONADE

1. Control; restriction
2. Enter; come through
3. Annoyed
4. Noble
5. Surly
6. Rotten; foul
7. Guard
8. Druggist; pharmacist
9. Small cannon
10. Peaceful
11. Brilliant
12. Mournful
13. Shamed; embarrassed
14. Guilty party
15. Disease
16. Wailing; mourning

A=	B=	C=	D=
E=	F=	G=	H=
I=	J=	K=	L=
M=	N=	O=	P=

85
Copyrighted

Slave Dancer Vocabulary Magic Squares 4 Answer Key

Match the definition with the vocabulary word. Put your answers in the magic squares below. When your answers are correct, all columns and rows will add to the same number.

A. APOTHECARY
B. RESTRAINT
C. MORTIFIED
D. MELANCHOLY
E. INGENIOUS
F. CULPRIT
G. PENETRATE
H. SENTINEL
I. TRANQUIL
J. AFFLICTION
K. CHAGRINED
L. RANCID
M. BROCADE
N. LOFTY
O. KEENING
P. CARRONADE

1. Control; restriction
2. Enter; come through
3. Annoyed
4. Noble
5. Surly
6. Rotten; foul
7. Guard
8. Druggist; pharmacist
9. Small cannon
10. Peaceful
11. Brilliant
12. Mournful
13. Shamed; embarrassed
14. Guilty party
15. Disease
16. Wailing; mourning

A=8	B=1	C=13	D=12
E=11	F=14	G=2	H=7
I=10	J=15	K=3	L=6
M=5	N=4	O=16	P=9

Slave Dancer Vocabulary Word Search 1

```
R A N C I D E N O T S Y L O H F L Q D R
B S E X H X X D E E K T C V M A E E V
R E L D N A H C N B F R M T C V T M T
B R I N Y C O T V V R O G R D A F R I Z
J G F D V M I S I F U L O E R R L A R D
R J E D E N N Q S W C M S P X R O W G P
S E D F E F J N A L S A E K S O G H E B
I D V L M D I S G J B D X Z T N G T B Y
M R R I T L Y E E E O K Y Z Z A E A A W
P E L I V D O L D R U M S E L D D A R N
E P S U O I N E G N I M U X N E Q K M D
N Z H Z P D F B C M S U O I T P A C A Z
E G V H L U M I N O U S R Y Y R P S M T
T N E M A L Y L E V I T C E L F E R E H
R U O Y S R X M M D H S I S E W Y G N V
A C R L P U R G A G H R D N V T A D T Q
B U E B H L R O I R R P U P I U D E J V
L L I A U Q A L W D T R L V S E E M D G
E P C I S L P C Y I O I S N W S E P Z
Q R O M R S E D I M N T A Q E R S N L N
D I B A G P N N A D S G J L P A U T U X
Z T A X V R H L T E L Y L C Z C R E M V
K P C N L Y C B F J S Y T T K K T D B V
```

Absolute; exact (5)
Arms; weapons (8)
Boldly resisted (6)
Brilliant (9)
Candle and supplies trader (8)
Celebration (9)
Confuses (6)
Confusion; disorder (5)
Corrupted (8)
Crazy; mad (8)
Crosswise; at right angles to the ship's keel (7)
Deadly; fatal (6)
Deliberately; with meaning (12)
Dense; too thick to go through (12)
Dishonorable (7)
Ease; relieve (7)
Faultfinding (8)
Foul (5)
Frightening (9)
Glowing; radiant (8)
Grimy; filthy (8)
Guard (8)
Guilty party (7)
Gully; ravine (6)
Lashed; whipped (7)

Limber; agile (4)
Military; warlike (7)
Noble (5)
Peacefully (8)
Pictured (9)
Pleasantly (7)
Portuguese slave broker (9)
Region of calm winds near the equator (8)
Rekindled; revived (10)
Revolts; uprisings (8)
Ridiculous (9)
Roaring; blustery (9)
Rotten (6)
Salty (5)
Scrubbed clean by a soft sandstone (10)
Seaweed (5)
Small cannon (9)
Sorry situation (6)
Testy (5)
Thoughtfully (9)
Tied up (7)
Unknown; unfamiliar (7)
Uproar (6)
Wail; sob (6)
Wretched; foul (4)

Slave Dancer Vocabulary Word Search 1 Answer Key

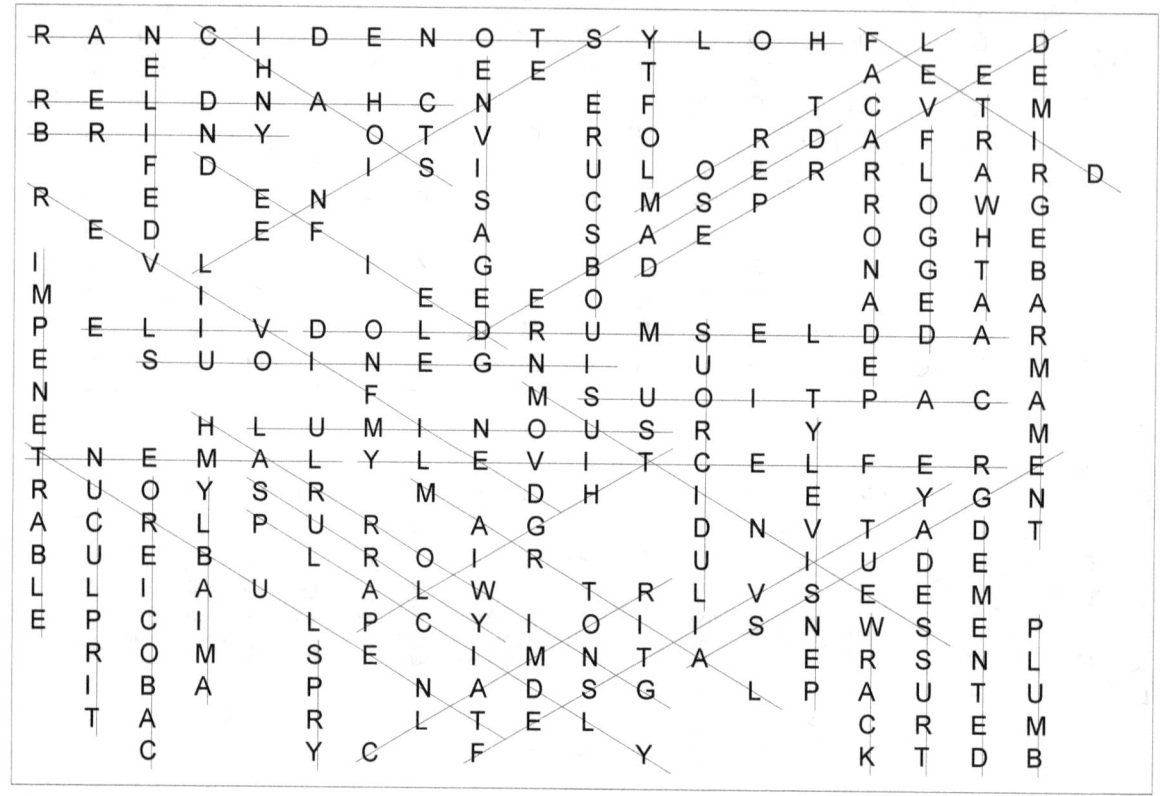

Absolute; exact (5)
Arms; weapons (8)
Boldly resisted (6)
Brilliant (9)
Candle and supplies trader (8)
Celebration (9)
Confuses (6)
Confusion; disorder (5)
Corrupted (8)
Crazy; mad (8)
Crosswise; at right angles to the ship's keel (7)
Deadly; fatal (6)
Deliberately; with meaning (12)
Dense; too thick to go through (12)
Dishonorable (7)
Ease; relieve (7)
Faultfinding (8)
Foul (5)
Frightening (9)
Glowing; radiant (8)
Grimy; filthy (8)
Guard (8)
Guilty party (7)
Gully; ravine (6)
Lashed; whipped (7)

Limber; agile (4)
Military; warlike (7)
Noble (5)
Peacefully (8)
Pictured (9)
Pleasantly (7)
Portuguese slave broker (9)
Region of calm winds near the equator (8)
Rekindled; revived (10)
Revolts; uprisings (8)
Ridiculous (9)
Roaring; blustery (9)
Rotten (6)
Salty (5)
Scrubbed clean by a soft sandstone (10)
Seaweed (5)
Small cannon (9)
Sorry situation (6)
Testy (5)
Thoughtfully (9)
Tied up (7)
Unknown; unfamiliar (7)
Uproar (6)
Wail; sob (6)
Wretched; foul (4)

Slave Dancer Vocabulary Word Search 2

```
P E N S I V E L Y S C G C J P P K D P Y
E T L G N N E E K V A E G Y C L E L D
R R S U O I M U L W T R R A P P M A N
I T M S N I D L L T G G R Y D K E C V
L Q L H G D B D I X F W P O T J N I D
O X A U Z S F E S P G E M Y H N Y T D K
U O R F D T M O L W L T N O L L A E L H
S U S T A I N E D E F I L E R O X D Y B
T E L Y R N C P L E R D G U K T F S E Z
A T N G X C D R N B C E S H D X A M B
G R E T S T G Z O L R A C S T X S L Y E
F B M D I T C X O U C P L I O U S V Z
D E V A N N K W C N S R L N S S I X D
R X S E M K E S A D Y O U X T S T Y M M
Q E M T Q E B L R E A M M N J A L U E G
C A V A I O N P R T S A B R R B T N D
L U I I T N J T A E S L C A I A I E J
D D L M V H I P B R U C U N N W K O C N
E X E P P I W T Y R A L M I C O C W P N
F Z G Y R A F A Y Y E G A E H R I B I V H
I S R R M I L I R D E S O R M Z N T D Q
E K B X L V T E E T D L A I A D D L E S
D B R O C A D E D D Y H M A R T I A L D
```

Abandon; get rid of (8)
Absolute; exact (5)
Arms; weapons (8)
Beheading (12)
Boldly resisted (6)
Celebration (9)
Confuses (6)
Confusion; disorder (5)
Crazy; mad (8)
Crosswise; at right angles to the ship's keel (7)
Dangerous (8)
Deadly; fatal (6)
Ease; relieve (7)
Elaborate woven fabric with a raised design (7)
Enclosure of slaves (9)
Faultfinding (8)
Fenced in (7)
Foul (5)
Frightening (9)
Glowing; radiant (8)
Grimy; filthy (8)
Guard (8)
Guilty party (7)
Gully; ravine (6)
Imitated (8)

Limber; agile (4)
Military; warlike (7)
Mournful (10)
Noble (5)
Peacefully (8)
Pleasantly (7)
Profitable (9)
Rekindled; revived (10)
Revolts; uprisings (8)
Ridiculous (9)
Rotten (6)
Salty (5)
Seaweed (5)
Small cannon (9)
Sorry situation (6)
Supported (9)
Testy (5)
Thoughtfully (9)
Unclear (10)
Unknown; unfamiliar (7)
Unstopped (10)
Uproar (6)
Wail; sob (6)
Wailing; mourning (7)
Wretched; foul (4)

Slave Dancer Vocabulary Word Search 2 Answer Key

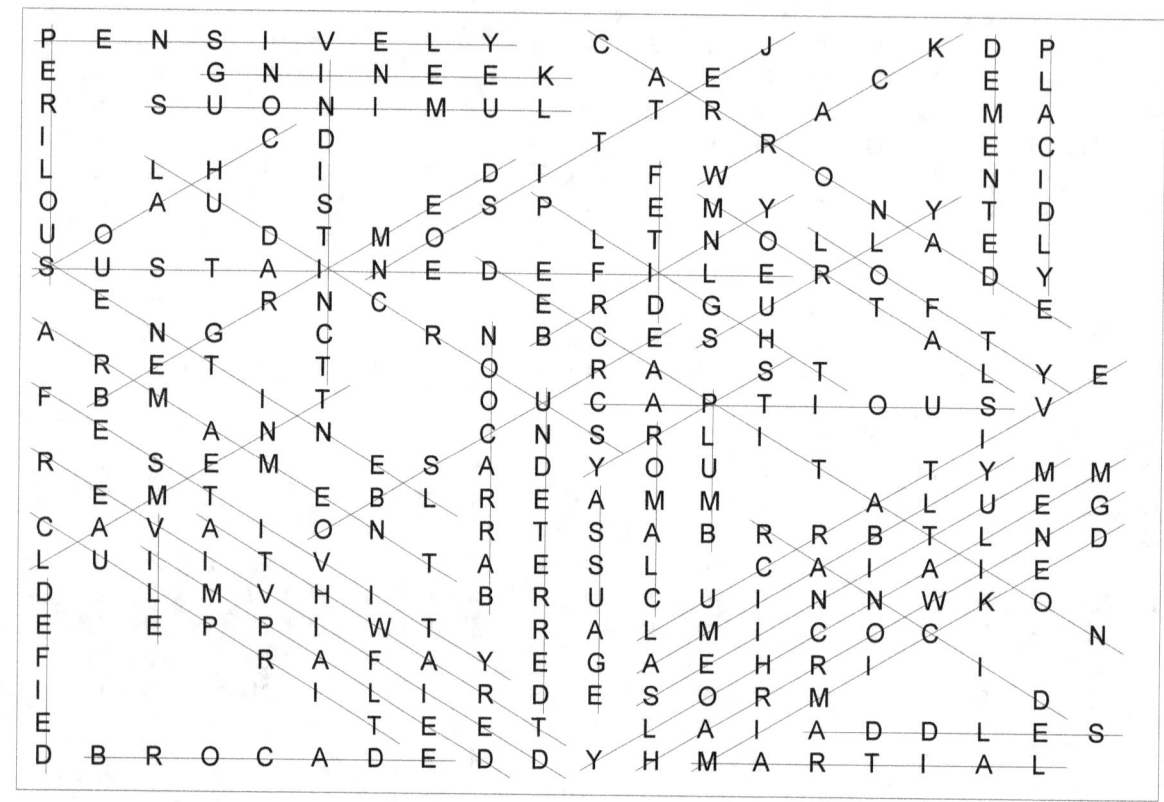

Abandon; get rid of (8)
Absolute; exact (5)
Arms; weapons (8)
Beheading (12)
Boldly resisted (6)
Celebration (9)
Confuses (6)
Confusion; disorder (5)
Crazy; mad (8)
Crosswise; at right angles to the ship's keel (7)
Dangerous (8)
Deadly; fatal (6)
Ease; relieve (7)
Elaborate woven fabric with a raised design (7)
Enclosure of slaves (9)
Faultfinding (8)
Fenced in (7)
Foul (5)
Frightening (9)
Glowing; radiant (8)
Grimy; filthy (8)
Guard (8)
Guilty party (7)
Gully; ravine (6)
Imitated (8)

Limber; agile (4)
Military; warlike (7)
Mournful (10)
Noble (5)
Peacefully (8)
Pleasantly (7)
Profitable (9)
Rekindled; revived (10)
Revolts; uprisings (8)
Ridiculous (9)
Rotten (6)
Salty (5)
Seaweed (5)
Small cannon (9)
Sorry situation (6)
Supported (9)
Testy (5)
Thoughtfully (9)
Unclear (10)
Unknown; unfamiliar (7)
Unstopped (10)
Uproar (6)
Wail; sob (6)
Wailing; mourning (7)
Wretched; foul (4)

Slave Dancer Vocabulary Word Search 3

```
C A R R O N A D E G A S I V N E Z A F W
H Y Q E V C Y E Q I R F W Z W V N M L R
F S Y S D R L N V M C Z Z D T O I O P
A K P T D T W C I D P A O P L V L S A G G
L A T R O M L A E A M N L I U I B G W
O N D A Y E J T S L E V I L A C T L E K
O B E I S T C S A E N U G E G R A T Y D X
F H P N B U U S A B D T L H V G A E I J N
N O R T P A R S S E K V S T I R T J M O B
E L A Z G L Z L D D M I V T I I O I T N
S Y V E C H K P Y E G O B C E V B M D S
S T E C L A M O R X Z N V E V E S I P T
C D D X Q F T N E M A L L E X C C E Y
Y O G E K Y E V N N L S B Y F D N U K N R
L N N I T P T O W P A S A E A Y R E E H
D E I F I V I V E R B E G R I M E D T Y
I D O E O S D S T E A N A A R Z H H R Q
C L Q D U U B E B P I C E D N A Q N A Y
A M X F S E N T I N E L K C D G C N T L
L T O Q P E Y D E P I D L N H L E O E Y
P R C Z P W V E I F P L U M B A E D S R N
P G Y M N V K K E N B R I N Y N O S S E
L A I T R A M D S S G Y T I V I T S E F
```

ADDLES	DEPRAVED	PERPLEXED
AFFLICTION	ENVISAGED	PLACIDLY
AGGRIEVED	FESTIVITY	PLIGHT
ALOOFNESS	FETID	PLUMB
AMIABLY	FLOGGED	PRESSGANGED
ARMAMENT	HOLYSTONED	PROFUSION
ASSUAGE	IMPALED	RANCID
BARRACOON	IMPENETRABLE	REFLECTIVELY
BEGRIMED	JETTISON	RESTRAINT
BRINY	KEENING	REVIVIFIED
CARRONADE	LAMENT	SENTINEL
CHAOS	LOFTY	SPRY
CLAMOR	LUCRATIVE	SURLY
CONFOUNDING	MARTIAL	SUSTAINED
CONVULSION	MIMICKED	VILE
DEBASED	MORTAL	WRACK
DEFIED	OBSCURE	
DEFILE	PENETRATE	

Slave Dancer Vocabulary Word Search 3 Answer Key

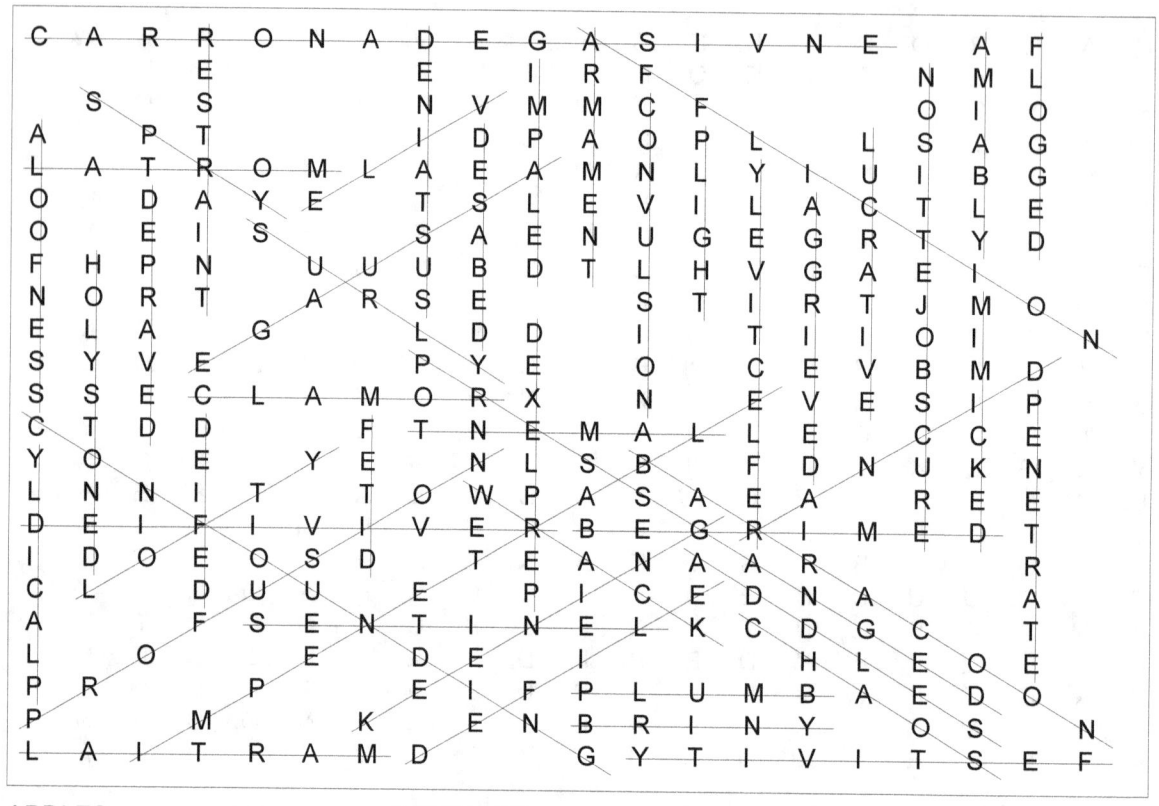

ADDLES	DEPRAVED	PERPLEXED
AFFLICTION	ENVISAGED	PLACIDLY
AGGRIEVED	FESTIVITY	PLIGHT
ALOOFNESS	FETID	PLUMB
AMIABLY	FLOGGED	PRESSGANGED
ARMAMENT	HOLYSTONED	PROFUSION
ASSUAGE	IMPALED	RANCID
BARRACOON	IMPENETRABLE	REFLECTIVELY
BEGRIMED	JETTISON	RESTRAINT
BRINY	KEENING	REVIVIFIED
CARRONADE	LAMENT	SENTINEL
CHAOS	LOFTY	SPRY
CLAMOR	LUCRATIVE	SURLY
CONFOUNDING	MARTIAL	SUSTAINED
CONVULSION	MIMICKED	VILE
DEBASED	MORTAL	WRACK
DEFIED	OBSCURE	
DEFILE	PENETRATE	

Slave Dancer Vocabulary Word Search 4

```
V N S U O L I R E P C M A R T I A L J J
F E D I D D E E A K S R Q B L U E C
L D E F L E S P L V R Q F R C T Q
C A K N D K V T G N I W O R A H R M
M H N N L H I R S N H D Z N D V X
Y K A G S O V A N T P W Q C Q D P T S D
U H V G U A M I B L Y I U W L U O S
C N W S R O W N L H U D S K I E N V Z
D M D W D I R T F E M L U X L S C P T
E E Z I E Q N O P Q B U S T W B H D M
F L O G G E N Y D U S D T R S A A V
I A M A A N Y D J I R E H R R M C M
E N I S S M I Z J I C I V A R I E D K
D C M S I A L F D N K R N M A T N H
E H I U V R F E I G V O E V B C A L B
I O C A N M V F C E J U D I L O B E Y
F L K G E A B K L N D S Y F I N E L T W
I Y E E R Y M E Z L I R O Y I N E L T G
T L D P Y E O O H O C R Z E G S R N B Z
R S E C N N F R M U P T G D A U E R Z
O D N I V T Y A T S Z J I B S M D T I Z
M N N X Y K L C H A O S E O A L H C N Z
C G B R O C A D E J L D Y L N Z Q N Y L
```

ADDLES	DEMENTED	MORTAL
AFFLICTION	DEPRAVED	MORTIFIED
AMIABLY	ENVISAGED	PERILOUS
ARMAMENT	FETID	PLACIDLY
ASSUAGE	FLOGGED	PLUMB
ATHWART	HARROWING	RANCID
BARRACOON	INGENIOUS	RELINQUISH
BRINY	JETTISON	RESTRAINT
BROCADE	KEENING	REVIVIFIED
CAPTIOUS	LAMENT	SHAMBLING
CHAGRINED	LANGUOROUS	SPRY
CHANDLER	LOFTY	SURLY
CHAOS	LUCRATIVE	SUSTAINED
CLAMOR	LUDICROUS	UNCHARITABLE
DEBASED	MARTIAL	UNDIGNIFIED
DEFIED	MELANCHOLY	VILE
DEFILE	MIMICKED	WRACK

Slave Dancer Vocabulary Word Search 4 Answer Key

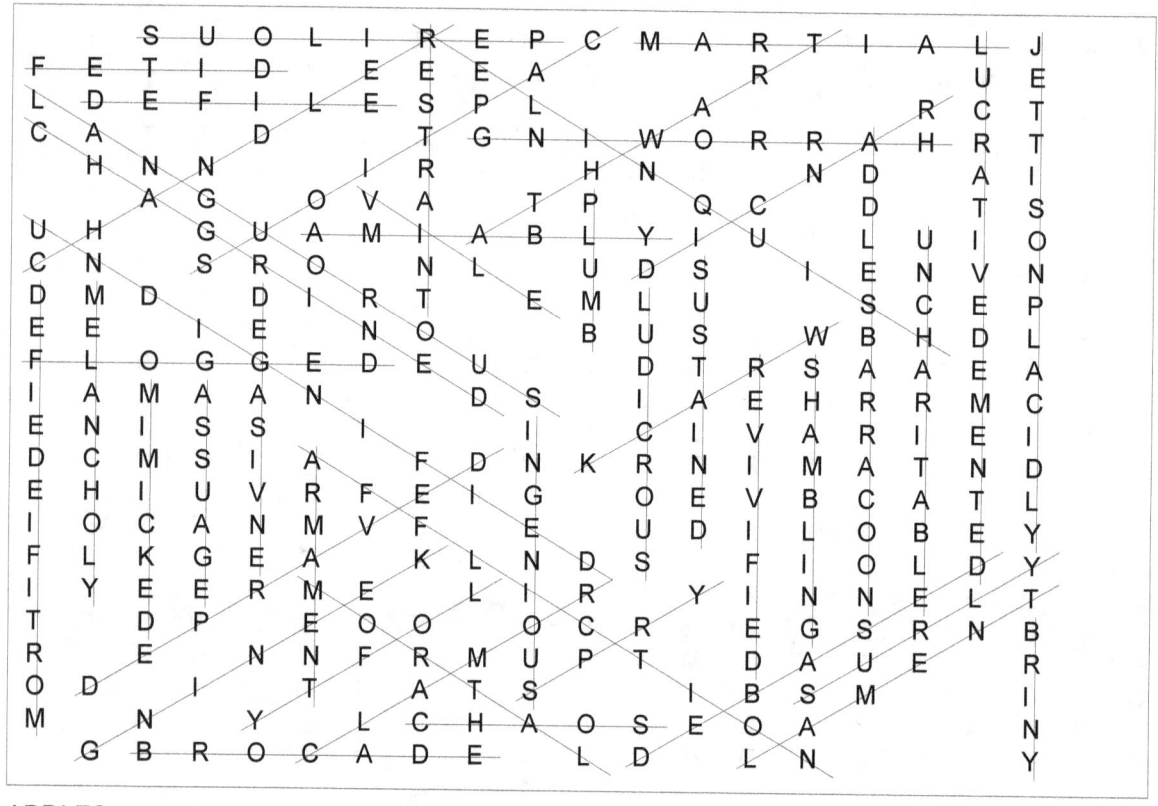

ADDLES	DEMENTED	MORTAL
AFFLICTION	DEPRAVED	MORTIFIED
AMIABLY	ENVISAGED	PERILOUS
ARMAMENT	FETID	PLACIDLY
ASSUAGE	FLOGGED	PLUMB
ATHWART	HARROWING	RANCID
BARRACOON	INGENIOUS	RELINQUISH
BRINY	JETTISON	RESTRAINT
BROCADE	KEENING	REVIVIFIED
CAPTIOUS	LAMENT	SHAMBLING
CHAGRINED	LANGUOROUS	SPRY
CHANDLER	LOFTY	SURLY
CHAOS	LUCRATIVE	SUSTAINED
CLAMOR	LUDICROUS	UNCHARITABLE
DEBASED	MARTIAL	UNDIGNIFIED
DEFIED	MELANCHOLY	VILE
DEFILE	MIMICKED	WRACK

Slave Dancer Vocabulary Crossword 1

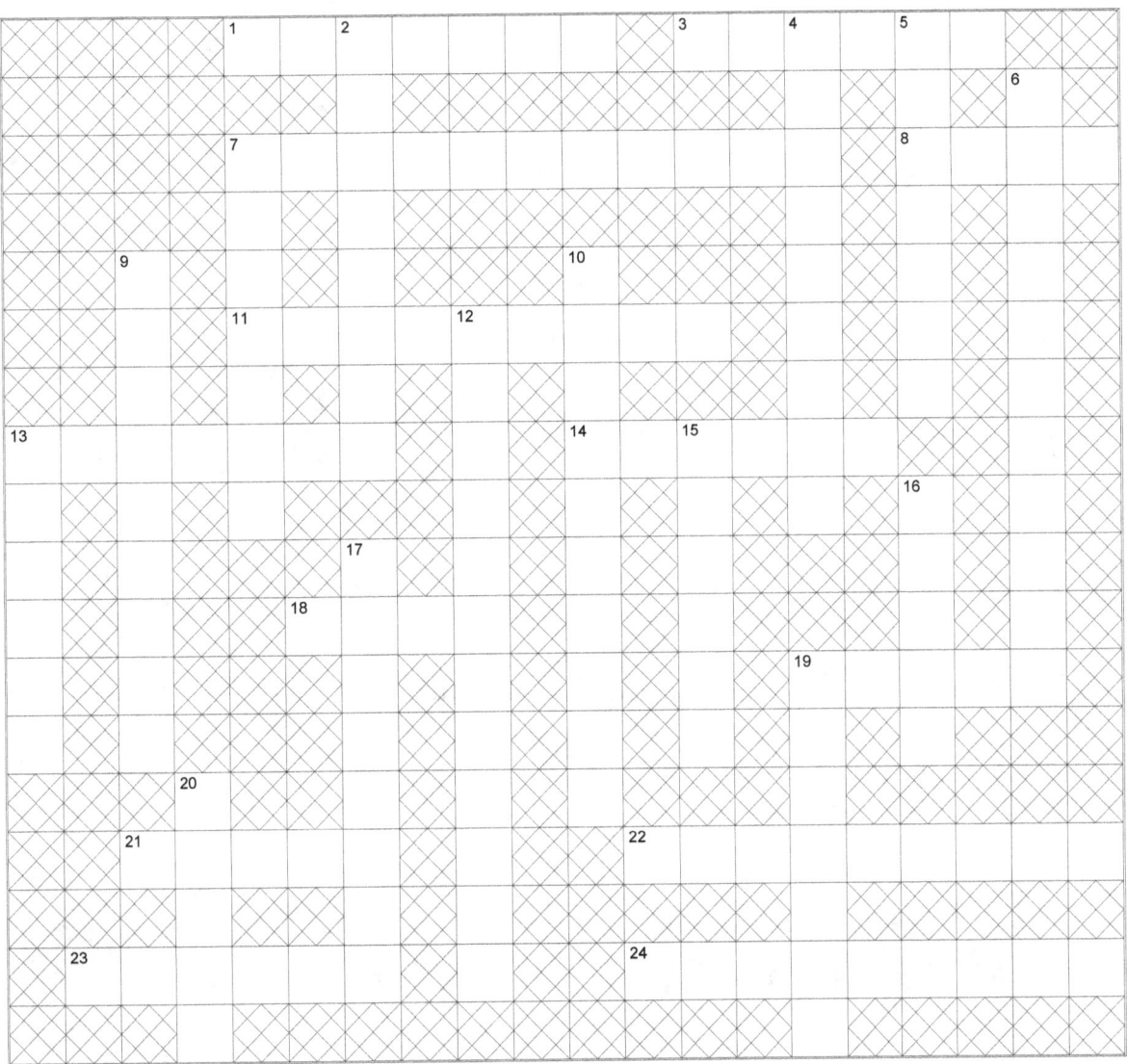

Across
1. Ease; relieve
3. Uproar
7. Puzzling; flustering
8. Limber; agile
11. Thoughtfully
13. Military; warlike
14. Confuses
18. Wretched; foul
19. Foul
21. Seaweed
22. Annoyed
23. Rotten
24. Enter; come through

Down
2. Guard
4. Pained
5. Unknown; unfamiliar
6. Forced into ship service
7. Guilty party
9. Frightening
10. Mournful
12. Dense; too thick to go through
13. Deadly; fatal
15. Boldly resisted
16. Noble
17. Imitated
19. Lashed; whipped
20. Salty

Slave Dancer Vocabulary Crossword 1 Answer Key

Across
1. Ease; relieve
3. Uproar
7. Puzzling; flustering
8. Limber; agile
11. Thoughtfully
13. Military; warlike
14. Confuses
18. Wretched; foul
19. Foul
21. Seaweed
22. Annoyed
23. Rotten
24. Enter; come through

Down
2. Guard
4. Pained
5. Unknown; unfamiliar
6. Forced into ship service
7. Guilty party
9. Frightening
10. Mournful
12. Dense; too thick to go through
13. Deadly; fatal
15. Boldly resisted
16. Noble
17. Imitated
19. Lashed; whipped
20. Salty

Slave Dancer Vocabulary Crossword 2

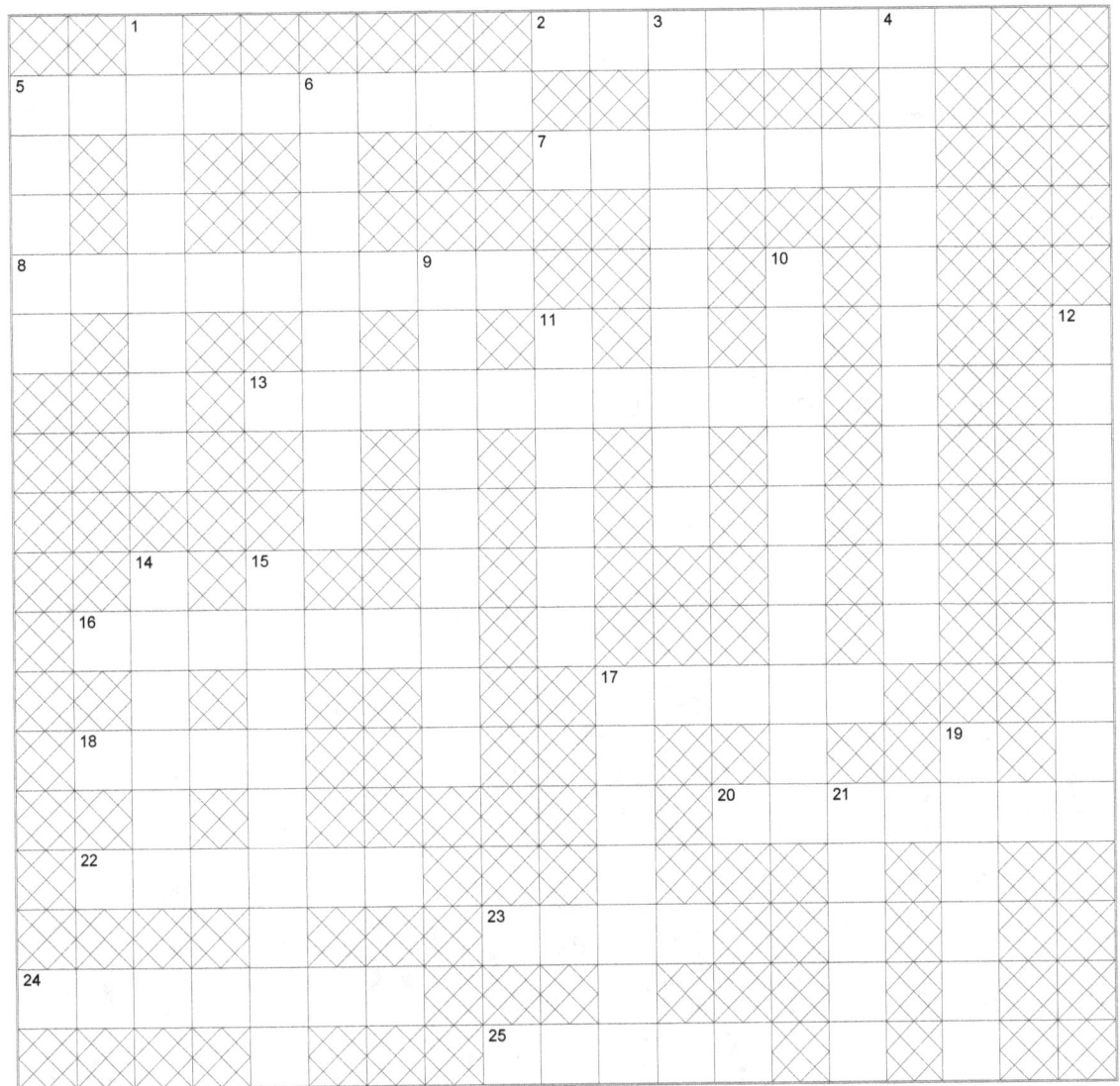

Across
2. Faultfinding
5. Charming or coaxing; flattering
7. Lashed; whipped
8. Annoyed
13. Contraction; shaking
16. Wailing; mourning
17. Confusion; disorder
18. Wretched; foul
20. Ease; relieve
22. Boldly resisted
23. Limber; agile
24. Unknown; unfamiliar
25. Foul

Down
1. Corrupted
3. Excess
4. Tasteless
5. Seaweed
6. Glowing; radiant
9. Pictured
10. Sleepy; lazy
11. Sorry situation
12. Profitable
14. Gully; ravine
15. Brilliant
17. Guilty party
19. Wail; sob
21. Testy

Slave Dancer Vocabulary Crossword 2 Answer Key

Across
2. Faultfinding
5. Charming or coaxing; flattering
7. Lashed; whipped
8. Annoyed
13. Contraction; shaking
16. Wailing; mourning
17. Confusion; disorder
18. Wretched; foul
20. Ease; relieve
22. Boldly resisted
23. Limber; agile
24. Unknown; unfamiliar
25. Foul

Down
1. Corrupted
3. Excess
4. Tasteless
5. Seaweed
6. Glowing; radiant
9. Pictured
10. Sleepy; lazy
11. Sorry situation
12. Profitable
14. Gully; ravine
15. Brilliant
17. Guilty party
19. Wail; sob
21. Testy

Slave Dancer Vocabulary Crossword 3

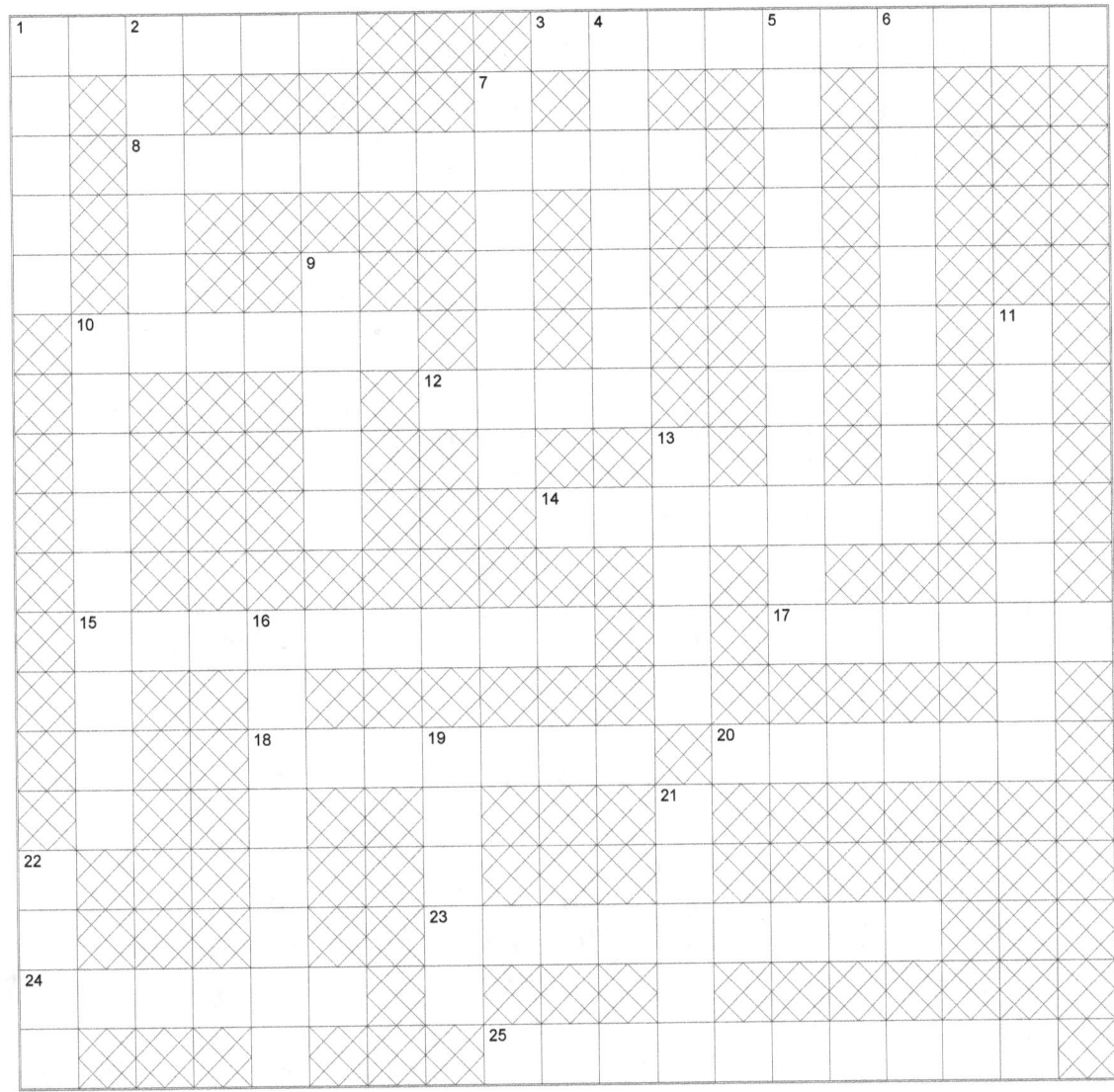

Across
1. Wail; sob
3. Contraction; shaking
8. Give up
10. Sorry situation
12. Wretched; foul
14. Wailing; mourning
15. Supported
17. Gully; ravine
18. Crosswise; at right angles to the ship's keel
20. Uproar
23. Annoyed
24. Rotten
25. Scrubbed clean by a soft sandstone

Down
1. Noble
2. Deadly; fatal
4. Unknown; unfamiliar
5. Tasteless
6. Shuffling
7. Guilty party
9. Confusion; disorder
10. Excess
11. Candle and supplies trader
13. Foul
16. Calm
19. Seaweed
21. Testy
22. Limber; agile

Slave Dancer Vocabulary Crossword 3 Answer Key

	1 L	2 A	M	E	N	T			3 C	4 O	N	V	5 U	L	6 S	I	O	N
	O		O					7 C		B			N		H			
	F		8 R	E	L	I	N	Q	U	I	S	H		D		A		
	T		T					L		C				I		M		
	Y		A		9 C			P		U				G		B		
		10 P	L	I	G	H	T		R		R			N		L		11 C
		R			A		12 V	I	L	E				I		I		H
		O			O			T				13 F		F		N		A
		F			S		14 K	E	E	N	I	N	G			D		N
		U						T		E								D
		15 S	U	16 S	T	A	I	N	E	D		17 D	E	F	I	L	E	
		I		R				D								E		
		18 O		A	T	H	19 W	A	R	T		20 C	L	A	M	O	R	
		N		N			R				21 S							
22 S				Q			A				U							
P				U			23 C	H	A	G	R	I	N	E	D			
24 R	A	N	C	I	D		K				L							
Y				L		25 H	O	L	Y	S	T	O	N	E	D			

Across
1. Wail; sob
3. Contraction; shaking
8. Give up
10. Sorry situation
12. Wretched; foul
14. Wailing; mourning
15. Supported
17. Gully; ravine
18. Crosswise; at right angles to the ship's keel
20. Uproar
23. Annoyed
24. Rotten
25. Scrubbed clean by a soft sandstone

Down
1. Noble
2. Deadly; fatal
4. Unknown; unfamiliar
5. Tasteless
6. Shuffling
7. Guilty party
9. Confusion; disorder
10. Excess
11. Candle and supplies trader
13. Foul
16. Calm
19. Seaweed
21. Testy
22. Limber; agile

Slave Dancer Vocabulary Crossword 4

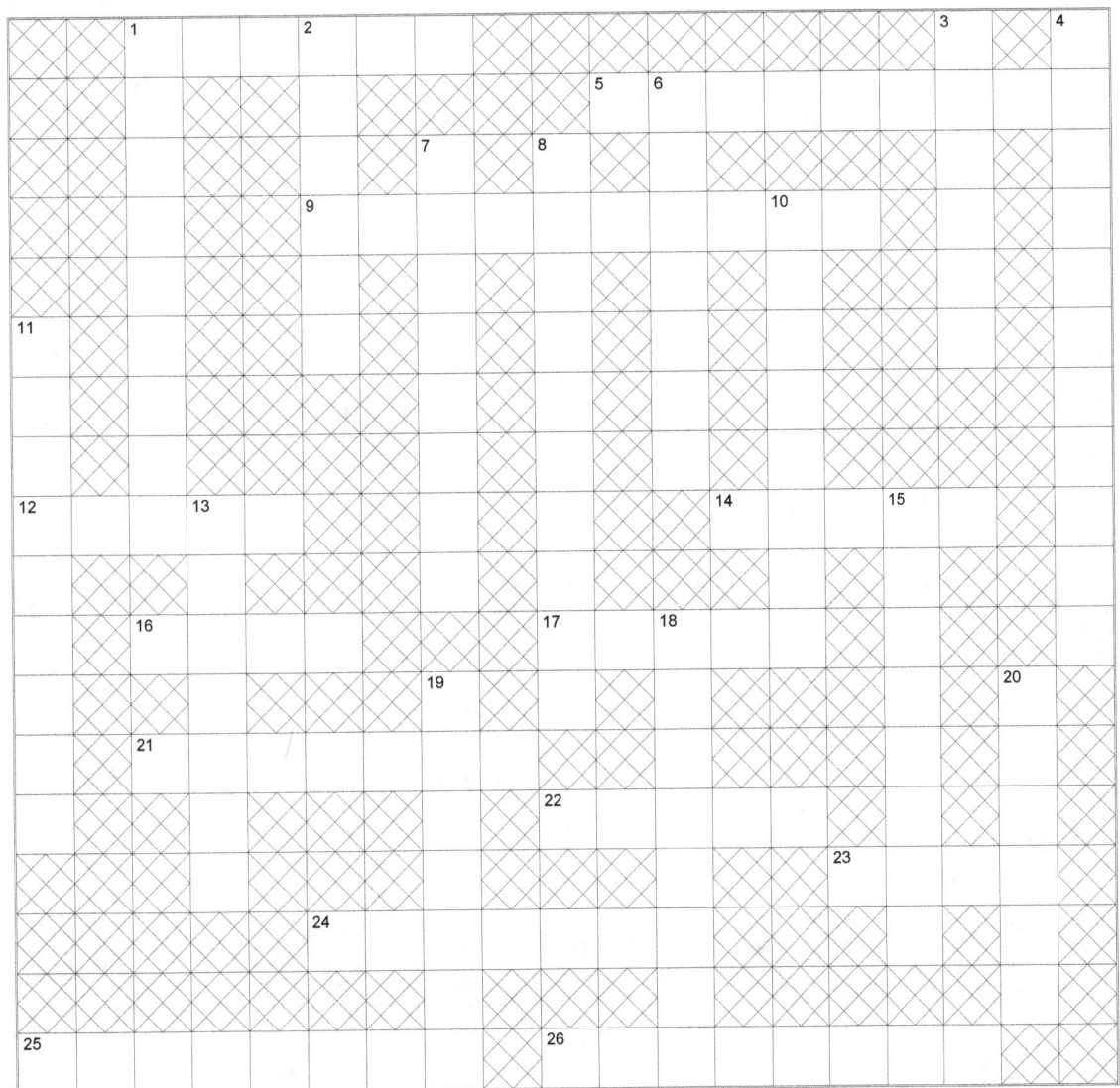

Across
1. Rotten
5. Portuguese slave broker
9. Mournful
12. Foul
14. Noble
16. Limber; agile
17. Confusion; disorder
21. Lashed; whipped
22. Seaweed
23. Wretched; foul
24. Unknown; unfamiliar
25. Imitated
26. Abandon; get rid of

Down
1. Leaning; idle
2. Uproar
3. Boldly resisted
4. Puzzling; flustering
6. Crosswise; at right angles to the ship's keel
7. Peacefully
8. Unclear
10. Glowing; radiant
11. Excess
13. Fenced in
15. Calm
18. Arms; weapons
19. Dishonorable
20. Wail; sob

Slave Dancer Vocabulary Crossword 4 Answer Key

Across
1. Rotten
5. Portuguese slave broker
9. Mournful
12. Foul
14. Noble
16. Limber; agile
17. Confusion; disorder
21. Lashed; whipped
22. Seaweed
23. Wretched; foul
24. Unknown; unfamiliar
25. Imitated
26. Abandon; get rid of

Down
1. Leaning; idle
2. Uproar
3. Boldly resisted
4. Puzzling; flustering
6. Crosswise; at right angles to the ship's keel
7. Peacefully
8. Unclear
10. Glowing; radiant
11. Excess
13. Fenced in
15. Calm
18. Arms; weapons
19. Dishonorable
20. Wail; sob

Slave Dancer Vocabulary Juggle Letters 1

1. TEUCBMERN = 1. _____
   Leaning; idle

2. TCIFAFILNO = 2. _____
   Disease

3. DCRANI = 3. _____
   Rotten; foul

4. SDADLE = 4. _____
   Confuses

5. NDIFNIDIEUG = 5. _____
   Tasteless

6. SSTEDRU = 6. _____
   Tied up

7. EGNHCADRI = 7. _____
   Annoyed

8. UBOESRC = 8. _____
   Unknown; unfamiliar

9. EDWGIELNH = 9. _____
   Charming or coaxing; flattering

10. TIMARLA =10. _____
    Military; warlike

11. DLRENACH =11. _____
    Candle and supplies merchant

12. YIPDLLAC =12. _____
    Peacefully

13. IMEMCKID =13. _____
    Imitated

14. AENPETETR =14. _____
    Enter; come through

15. VDGGRIAEE =15. _____
    Pained

Slave Dancer Vocabulary Juggle Letters 1 Answer Key

1. TEUCBMERN = 1. RECUMBENT
   Leaning; idle

2. TCIFAFILNO = 2. AFFLICTION
   Disease

3. DCRANI = 3. RANCID
   Rotten; foul

4. SDADLE = 4. ADDLES
   Confuses

5. NDIFNIDIEUG = 5. UNDIGNIFIED
   Tasteless

6. SSTEDRU = 6. TRUSSED
   Tied up

7. EGNHCADRI = 7. CHAGRINED
   Annoyed

8. UBOESRC = 8. OBSCURE
   Unknown; unfamiliar

9. EDWGIELNH = 9. WHEEDLING
   Charming or coaxing; flattering

10. TIMARLA = 10. MARTIAL
    Military; warlike

11. DLRENACH = 11. CHANDLER
    Candle and supplies merchant

12. YIPDLLAC = 12. PLACIDLY
    Peacefully

13. IMEMCKID = 13. MIMICKED
    Imitated

14. AENPETETR = 14. PENETRATE
    Enter; come through

15. VDGGRIAEE = 15. AGGRIEVED
    Pained

Slave Dancer Vocabulary Juggle Letters 2

1. EUTMIISN = 1. _____
   Revolts; uprisings

2. OALMTR = 2. _____
   Deadly; fatal

3. EETERANTP = 3. _____
   Enter; come through

4. RNBIY = 4. _____
   Salty sea water

5. OEIAOCRBC = 5. _____
   Portuguese slave broker

6. NDTIINSTCI = 6. _____
   Unclear

7. NEDALHCR = 7. _____
   Candle and supplies merchant

8. EINROTSSOTATP = 8. _____
   Objections

9. AVEEGSIN = 9. _____
   Picture

10. NDCRAI =10. _____
    Rotten; foul

11. TYFLO =11. _____
    Noble

12. SUOMUNIL =12. _____
    Glowing radiant

13. YAETRAPOCH =13. _____
    Druggist; pharmacist

14. NSDTUSEAI =14. _____
    Supported

15. NTEIENSL =15. _____
    Guard

Slave Dancer Vocabulary Juggle Letters 2 Answer Key

1. EUTMIISN = 1. MUTINIES
   Revolts; uprisings
2. OALMTR = 2. MORTAL
   Deadly; fatal
3. EETERANTP = 3. PENETRATE
   Enter; come through
4. RNBIY = 4. BRINY
   Salty sea water
5. OEIAOCRBC = 5. CABOCIERO
   Portuguese slave broker
6. NDTIINSTCI = 6. INDISTINCT
   Unclear
7. NEDALHCR = 7. CHANDLER
   Candle and supplies merchant
8. EINROTSSOTATP = 8. PROTESTATIONS
   Objections
9. AVEEGSIN = 9. ENVISAGE
   Picture
10. NDCRAI =10. RANCID
    Rotten; foul
11. TYFLO =11. LOFTY
    Noble
12. SUOMUNIL =12. LUMINOUS
    Glowing radiant
13. YAETRAPOCH =13. APOTHECARY
    Druggist; pharmacist
14. NSDTUSEAI =14. SUSTAINED
    Supported
15. NTEIENSL =15. SENTINEL
    Guard

Slave Dancer Vocabulary Juggle Letters 3

1. MUBLP = 1. _____
Absolute; exact

2. DDIUFNGEINI = 2. _____
Tasteless

3. YACPLLID = 3. _____
Peacefully

4. DEIEFD = 4. _____
Boldly resisted

5. EDSOYHTOLN = 5. _____
Scrubbed clean by a soft sandstone

6. RAOLMT = 6. _____
Deadly; fatal

7. IARNCGDEH = 7. _____
Annoyed

8. OSCHA = 8. _____
Confusion; disorder

9. OSIJTNET = 9. _____
Abandon; get rid of

10. MATELN = 10. _____
Wail; sob

11. RBTUEUNLT = 11. _____
Roaring; blustery

12. BROSECU = 12. _____
Unknown; unfamiliar

13. EIDTF = 13. _____
Foul

14. LTUCRPI = 14. _____
Guilty party

15. RPENSSDAGGE = 15. _____
Forced onto ship service

Slave Dancer Vocabulary Juggle Letters 3 Answer Key

1. MUBLP = 1. PLUMB
   Absolute; exact

2. DDIUFNGEINI = 2. UNDIGNIFIED
   Tasteless

3. YACPLLID = 3. PLACIDLY
   Peacefully

4. DEIEFD = 4. DEFIED
   Boldly resisted

5. EDSOYHTOLN = 5. HOLYSTONED
   Scrubbed clean by a soft sandstone

6. RAOLMT = 6. MORTAL
   Deadly; fatal

7. IARNCGDEH = 7. CHAGRINED
   Annoyed

8. OSCHA = 8. CHAOS
   Confusion; disorder

9. OSIJTNET = 9. JETTISON
   Abandon; get rid of

10. MATELN = 10. LAMENT
    Wail; sob

11. RBTUEUNLT = 11. TURBULENT
    Roaring; blustery

12. BROSECU = 12. OBSCURE
    Unknown; unfamiliar

13. EIDTF = 13. FETID
    Foul

14. LTUCRPI = 14. CULPRIT
    Guilty party

15. RPENSSDAGGE = 15. PRESSGANGED
    Forced onto ship service

Slave Dancer Vocabulary Juggle Letters 4

1. EAPEETNTR = 1. _____
   Enter; come through

2. IENMUITS = 2. _____
   Revolts; uprisings

3. UPIESLOR = 3. _____
   Dangerous

4. OHTNLOYESD = 4. _____
   Scrubbed clean by a soft sandstone

5. EREXPDELP = 5. _____
   Puzzled

6. HOCSA = 6. _____
   Confusion; disorder

7. DWHGNEELI = 7. _____
   Charming or coaxing; flattering

8. IFOALNICTF = 8. _____
   Disease

9. TIRLEBPEANEM = 9. _____
   Dense; thick

10. OARRCABNO =10. _____
    Enclosure of slaves

11. UEASAGS =11. _____
    Ease; relieve

12. NLVUOICSNO =12. _____
    Contraction; shaking

13. RSUDSTE =13. _____
    Tied up

14. IGEINSUON =14. _____
    Brilliant

15. RDROACENA =15. _____
    Small cannon

Slave Dancer Vocabulary Juggle Letters 4 Answer Key

1. EAPEETNTR = 1. PENETRATE
   Enter; come through

2. IENMUITS = 2. MUTINIES
   Revolts; uprisings

3. UPIESLOR = 3. PERILOUS
   Dangerous

4. OHTNLOYESD = 4. HOLYSTONED
   Scrubbed clean by a soft sandstone

5. EREXPDELP = 5. PERPLEXED
   Puzzled

6. HOCSA = 6. CHAOS
   Confusion; disorder

7. DWHGNEELI = 7. WHEEDLING
   Charming or coaxing; flattering

8. IFOALNICTF = 8. AFFLICTION
   Disease

9. TIRLEBPEANEM = 9. IMPENETRABLE
   Dense; thick

10. OARRCABNO = 10. BARRACOON
    Enclosure of slaves

11. UEASAGS = 11. ASSUAGE
    Ease; relieve

12. NLVUOICSNO = 12. CONVULSION
    Contraction; shaking

13. RSUDSTE = 13. TRUSSED
    Tied up

14. IGEINSUON = 14. INGENIOUS
    Brilliant

15. RDROACENA = 15. CARRONADE
    Small cannon

ADDLES	Confuses
AFFLICTION	Disease
AGGRIEVED	Pained
ALOOFNESS	Indifference
AMIABLY	Pleasantly
APOTHECARY	Druggist; pharmacist

ARMAMENT	Arms; weapons
ASSUAGE	Ease; relieve
ATHWART	Crosswise; at right angles with the ship's keel
BARBAROUSNESS	Horribly cruel
BARRACOON	Enclosure of slaves
BEGRIMED	Grimy; filthy

BRINY	Salty sea water
BROCADE	Surly
CABOCIERO	Portuguese slave broker
CAPTIOUS	Faultfinding
CARRONADE	Small cannon
CHAGRINED	Annoyed

CHANDLER	Candle and supplies merchant
CHAOS	Confusion; disorder
CLAMOR	Uproar
CONFOUNDING	Puzzling; flustering
CONVULSION	Contraction; shaking
CULPRIT	Guilty party

DEBASED	Dishonorable
DECAPITATION	Beheading
DEFIED	Boldly resisted
DEFILE	Gully; ravine
DEMENTED	Crazy; mad
DEPRAVED	Corrupted

DOLDRUMS	Region of calm winds near the equator
ENVISAGE	Picture
FESTIVITY	Celebration
FETID	Foul
FLOGGED	Lashed; whipped
HARROWING	Frightening

HOLYSTONED	Scrubbed clean by a soft sandstone
IMPALED	Fenced in
IMPASSIVELY	Without expression
IMPENETRABLE	Dense; thick
IMPERTINENT	Sassy; fresh
INDISTINCT	Unclear

INGENIOUS	Brilliant
JETTISON	Abandon; get rid of
KEENING	Wailing; mourning
LAMENT	Wail; sob
LANGUOROUS	Sleepy; lazy
LOFTY	Noble

LUCRATIVE	Profitable
LUDICROUS	Ridiculous
LUMINOUS	Glowing radiant
MARTIAL	Military; warlike
MELANCHOLY	Mournful
MIMICKED	Imitated

MORTAL	Deadly; fatal
MORTIFIED	Shamed; embarrassed
MUTINIES	Revolts; uprisings
OBSCURE	Unknown; unfamiliar
PENETRATE	Enter; come through
PENSIVELY	Thoughtfully

PERILOUS	Dangerous
PERPLEXED	Puzzled
PLACIDLY	Peacefully
PLIGHT	Sorry situation
PLUMB	Absolute; exact
PRESSGANGED	Forced onto ship service

PROFUSION	Excess
PROTESTATIONS	Objections
RANCID	Rotten; foul
RECUMBENT	Leaning; idle
REFLECTIVELY	Deliberately; with meaning
RELINQUISH	Give up

RESTRAINT	Control; restriction
REVIVIFIED	Rekindled; revived
SENTINEL	Guard
SHAMBLING	Shuffling
SPRY	Limber; agile
SUSTAINED	Supported

TRANQUIL	Peaceful
TRUSSED	Tied up
TURBULENT	Roaring; blustery
UNCHARITABLE	Hard hearted
UNDETERRED	Unstopped
UNDIGNIFIED	Tasteless

VILE	Foul
WHEEDLING	Charming or coaxing; flattering
WRACK	Seaweed

Slave Dancer Vocabulary

INDISTINCT	CHAGRINED	CLAMOR	SPRY	AMIABLY
UNDIGNIFIED	FETID	LUCRATIVE	RESTRAINT	ADDLES
CABOCIERO	KEENING	FREE SPACE	CULPRIT	PRESSGANGED
DOLDRUMS	UNDETERRED	TRUSSED	BARBAROUSNESS	TRANQUIL
PERPLEXED	VILE	IMPASSIVELY	SUSTAINED	PROFUSION

Slave Dancer Vocabulary

REVIVIFIED	BRINY	IMPALED	DEFIED	LUDICROUS
ASSUAGE	ARMAMENT	LAMENT	CAPTIOUS	IMPENETRABLE
SHAMBLING	BARRACOON	FREE SPACE	UNCHARITABLE	FESTIVITY
LANGOROUS	IMPERTINENT	JETTISON	AGGRIEVED	FLOGGED
PENETRATE	APOTHECARY	INGENIOUS	PLACIDLY	DECAPITATION

Slave Dancer Vocabulary

DOLDRUMS	BROCADE	PRESSGANGED	TRANQUIL	CULPRIT
AFFLICTION	PENETRATE	RANCID	CLAMOR	DEFIED
BEGRIMED	CONVULSION	FREE SPACE	FLOGGED	DEMENTED
CHAOS	MORTAL	IMPALED	REVIVIFIED	PROTESTATIONS
AGGRIEVED	CONFOUNDING	UNDIGNIFIED	ASSUAGE	LUCRATIVE

Slave Dancer Vocabulary

INDISTINCT	CABOCIERO	SHAMBLING	DEPRAVED	FESTIVITY
ADDLES	IMPENETRABLE	ATHWART	HOLYSTONED	APOTHECARY
LANGUOROUS	MIMICKED	FREE SPACE	BARRACOON	DECAPITATION
REFLECTIVELY	RECUMBENT	OBSCURE	CHANDLER	JETTISON
MARTIAL	FETID	CAPTIOUS	DEFILE	ALOOFNESS

Slave Dancer Vocabulary

ADDLES	RECUMBENT	DEFILE	DOLDRUMS	MORTAL
SHAMBLING	IMPERTINENT	TURBULENT	BARBAROUSNESS	LAMENT
DEMENTED	HARROWING	FREE SPACE	FLOGGED	LANGUOROUS
OBSCURE	DEBASED	ATHWART	CAPTIOUS	CHANDLER
HOLYSTONED	MORTIFIED	MIMICKED	PRESSGANGED	WHEEDLING

Slave Dancer Vocabulary

CLAMOR	ASSUAGE	AFFLICTION	SUSTAINED	IMPASSIVELY
CARRONADE	LUCRATIVE	KEENING	PERILOUS	BARRACOON
BROCADE	CHAGRINED	FREE SPACE	AMIABLY	UNCHARITABLE
REFLECTIVELY	SENTINEL	RESTRAINT	BEGRIMED	IMPENETRABLE
TRUSSED	PERPLEXED	RANCID	ENVISAGED	RELINQUISH

Slave Dancer Vocabulary

LOFTY	CARRONADE	PROTESTATIONS	MORTAL	FESTIVITY
AFFLICTION	RESTRAINT	PENETRATE	LAMENT	INGENIOUS
SPRY	TRUSSED	FREE SPACE	BEGRIMED	IMPALED
AMIABLY	DEMENTED	CHAOS	ALOOFNESS	CABOCIERO
MELANCHOLY	DEBASED	TRANQUIL	BARBAROUSNESS	UNDETERRED

Slave Dancer Vocabulary

SENTINEL	LUMINOUS	PERPLEXED	HARROWING	IMPASSIVELY
ENVISAGED	HOLYSTONED	REFLECTIVELY	REVIVIFIED	BROCADE
OBSCURE	LANGOROUS	FREE SPACE	LUCRATIVE	RELINQUISH
DEFIED	IMPENETRABLE	RANCID	SUSTAINED	DEFILE
FETID	CLAMOR	CHAGRINED	VILE	UNCHARITABLE

Slave Dancer Vocabulary

BRINY	APOTHECARY	PLIGHT	UNDETERRED	PROTESTATIONS
PENSIVELY	FESTIVITY	UNCHARITABLE	PERPLEXED	ASSUAGE
AGGRIEVED	TRUSSED	FREE SPACE	SHAMBLING	ALOOFNESS
ATHWART	ADDLES	CULPRIT	KEENING	DEBASED
CAPTIOUS	TRANQUIL	LUCRATIVE	OBSCURE	WHEEDLING

Slave Dancer Vocabulary

FLOGGED	DEPRAVED	RESTRAINT	DEMENTED	MELANCHOLY
DEFILE	VILE	LUMINOUS	REFLECTIVELY	CARRONADE
BARBAROUSNESS	SPRY	FREE SPACE	WRACK	UNDIGNIFIED
IMPENETRABLE	MORTIFIED	INGENIOUS	IMPASSIVELY	JETTISON
CONVULSION	LANGUOROUS	MIMICKED	CONFOUNDING	PERILOUS

Slave Dancer Vocabulary

BARBAROUSNESS	RANCID	PLACIDLY	SHAMBLING	PROFUSION
TURBULENT	LAMENT	ATHWART	ARMAMENT	INDISTINCT
DEFIED	FETID	FREE SPACE	CONFOUNDING	MORTAL
PENSIVELY	BROCADE	MIMICKED	CHANDLER	CULPRIT
PROTESTATIONS	LOFTY	FLOGGED	BEGRIMED	FESTIVITY

Slave Dancer Vocabulary

REFLECTIVELY	LUMINOUS	TRANQUIL	AFFLICTION	CARRONADE
OBSCURE	PERPLEXED	IMPENETRABLE	CABOCIERO	ALOOFNESS
DECAPITATION	UNDIGNIFIED	FREE SPACE	PENETRATE	IMPERTINENT
KEENING	TRUSSED	AGGRIEVED	APOTHECARY	CAPTIOUS
INGENIOUS	IMPALED	LUCRATIVE	LANGUOROUS	RECUMBENT

Slave Dancer Vocabulary

PROTESTATIONS	TURBULENT	DEMENTED	SENTINEL	CONFOUNDING
WHEEDLING	AFFLICTION	CAPTIOUS	RELINQUISH	SUSTAINED
CULPRIT	PERILOUS	FREE SPACE	KEENING	HARROWING
LAMENT	PLUMB	ATHWART	OBSCURE	JETTISON
PERPLEXED	MORTIFIED	MELANCHOLY	MIMICKED	MUTINIES

Slave Dancer Vocabulary

UNCHARITABLE	CONVULSION	HOLYSTONED	TRANQUIL	DEFILE
AGGRIEVED	FLOGGED	PENETRATE	PENSIVELY	IMPENETRABLE
AMIABLY	ASSUAGE	FREE SPACE	LUCRATIVE	DEBASED
LUDICROUS	MARTIAL	TRUSSED	SHAMBLING	CHANDLER
CLAMOR	CABOCIERO	DOLDRUMS	FETID	RESTRAINT

Slave Dancer Vocabulary

DEFILE	BARBAROUSNESS	AGGRIEVED	SUSTAINED	APOTHECARY
PLUMB	AMIABLY	BRINY	TURBULENT	AFFLICTION
BEGRIMED	ADDLES	FREE SPACE	ARMAMENT	SPRY
RECUMBENT	HOLYSTONED	REVIVIFIED	ENVISAGED	WHEEDLING
DEFIED	PROTESTATIONS	TRUSSED	IMPALED	BARRACOON

Slave Dancer Vocabulary

CARRONADE	ASSUAGE	DOLDRUMS	PERILOUS	IMPASSIVELY
FLOGGED	MIMICKED	CHANDLER	DEPRAVED	TRANQUIL
ALOOFNESS	ATHWART	FREE SPACE	LAMENT	RELINQUISH
CAPTIOUS	SHAMBLING	PENETRATE	LUCRATIVE	PERPLEXED
WRACK	UNCHARITABLE	UNDETERRED	CONVULSION	PRESSGANGED

Slave Dancer Vocabulary

CONVULSION	LUMINOUS	ASSUAGE	PRESSGANGED	REFLECTIVELY
MUTINIES	TRANQUIL	LUDICROUS	PENSIVELY	CULPRIT
FESTIVITY	TRUSSED	FREE SPACE	FETID	IMPASSIVELY
IMPERTINENT	KEENING	LANGUOROUS	ARMAMENT	LAMENT
AFFLICTION	HARROWING	PLUMB	DEFILE	ENVISAGED

Slave Dancer Vocabulary

BARRACOON	APOTHECARY	INDISTINCT	LOFTY	BROCADE
CAPTIOUS	DEFIED	TURBULENT	LUCRATIVE	IMPALED
PLACIDLY	IMPENETRABLE	FREE SPACE	CHAGRINED	BARBAROUSNESS
DEMENTED	UNDIGNIFIED	RESTRAINT	VILE	PENETRATE
RELINQUISH	BRINY	SENTINEL	UNDETERRED	CARRONADE

Slave Dancer Vocabulary

MARTIAL	INGENIOUS	CABOCIERO	IMPENETRABLE	CHAOS
UNDIGNIFIED	PLACIDLY	OBSCURE	MUTINIES	TRANQUIL
ADDLES	FESTIVITY	FREE SPACE	KEENING	RANCID
LUDICROUS	REVIVIFIED	TRUSSED	IMPASSIVELY	SENTINEL
PROTESTATIONS	ENVISAGED	PENETRATE	BARBAROUSNESS	PERPLEXED

Slave Dancer Vocabulary

REFLECTIVELY	DEFILE	MELANCHOLY	BEGRIMED	HARROWING
APOTHECARY	HOLYSTONED	CAPTIOUS	CULPRIT	VILE
CHAGRINED	UNDETERRED	FREE SPACE	DECAPITATION	RELINQUISH
FLOGGED	PLIGHT	ATHWART	DEPRAVED	LOFTY
CARRONADE	PROFUSION	CONVULSION	RECUMBENT	AMIABLY

Slave Dancer Vocabulary

CONVULSION	LANGUOROUS	PROTESTATIONS	CARRONADE	BARRACOON
CABOCIERO	REFLECTIVELY	DEPRAVED	CLAMOR	FETID
ALOOFNESS	MARTIAL	FREE SPACE	HARROWING	DOLDRUMS
UNDETERRED	SHAMBLING	AGGRIEVED	SUSTAINED	HOLYSTONED
AMIABLY	RECUMBENT	MELANCHOLY	IMPENETRABLE	TURBULENT

Slave Dancer Vocabulary

ASSUAGE	ADDLES	LUCRATIVE	BRINY	JETTISON
DEMENTED	REVIVIFIED	SENTINEL	ENVISAGED	DEFILE
PENETRATE	OBSCURE	FREE SPACE	CONFOUNDING	CULPRIT
TRUSSED	TRANQUIL	PERILOUS	INGENIOUS	CHAOS
UNCHARITABLE	WRACK	CHANDLER	FLOGGED	PLACIDLY

Slave Dancer Vocabulary

DOLDRUMS	CHAOS	CULPRIT	PERPLEXED	IMPENETRABLE
MIMICKED	UNDETERRED	BROCADE	IMPERTINENT	WRACK
TRANQUIL	REVIVIFIED	FREE SPACE	MARTIAL	PLACIDLY
ASSUAGE	INGENIOUS	LAMENT	MELANCHOLY	APOTHECARY
DEBASED	ADDLES	RESTRAINT	UNDIGNIFIED	CARRONADE

Slave Dancer Vocabulary

LANGUOROUS	PRESSGANGED	CABOCIERO	RELINQUISH	REFLECTIVELY
SPRY	PERILOUS	ENVISAGED	SUSTAINED	BRINY
VILE	DECAPITATION	FREE SPACE	OBSCURE	SENTINEL
ALOOFNESS	IMPALED	DEPRAVED	ATHWART	LUCRATIVE
SHAMBLING	HARROWING	BARBAROUSNESS	LOFTY	CONVULSION

Slave Dancer Vocabulary

PERPLEXED	PROTESTATIONS	CAPTIOUS	ENVISAGE	ASSUAGE
BRINY	AGGRIEVED	REFLECTIVELY	LUDICROUS	REVIVIFIED
IMPASSIVELY	CULPRIT	FREE SPACE	RESTRAINT	CABOCIERO
CHAOS	SPRY	ALOOFNESS	CHANDLER	ADDLES
SUSTAINED	INDISTINCT	DEBASED	PENETRATE	MIMICKED

Slave Dancer Vocabulary

TRANQUIL	LANGUOROUS	PENSIVELY	SHAMBLING	DEFILE
HOLYSTONED	CONFOUNDING	FLOGGED	LOFTY	PERILOUS
JETTISON	VILE	FREE SPACE	MORTIFIED	BARRACOON
SENTINEL	MELANCHOLY	AFFLICTION	BEGRIMED	ARMAMENT
IMPERTINENT	PLUMB	IMPALED	CONVULSION	RECUMBENT

Slave Dancer Vocabulary

MARTIAL	PROFUSION	DEBASED	SPRY	UNDIGNIFIED
REVIVIFIED	ADDLES	RECUMBENT	TURBULENT	SUSTAINED
ASSUAGE	LAMENT	FREE SPACE	CHAOS	PRESSGANGED
FESTIVITY	DEMENTED	MIMICKED	AMIABLY	CONVULSION
CONFOUNDING	IMPENETRABLE	MORTIFIED	RELINQUISH	CLAMOR

Slave Dancer Vocabulary

ARMAMENT	PERPLEXED	KEENING	PLACIDLY	BARRACOON
IMPASSIVELY	HARROWING	LUCRATIVE	BROCADE	AGGRIEVED
JETTISON	AFFLICTION	FREE SPACE	DEFIED	HOLYSTONED
MORTAL	DEPRAVED	RESTRAINT	LUDICROUS	BEGRIMED
DECAPITATION	LOFTY	CABOCIERO	FLOGGED	IMPERTINENT

Slave Dancer Vocabulary

ALOOFNESS	PROFUSION	OBSCURE	CABOCIERO	MUTINIES
BEGRIMED	SENTINEL	PLUMB	SPRY	MELANCHOLY
PLIGHT	CHAOS	FREE SPACE	IMPASSIVELY	CLAMOR
DOLDRUMS	WRACK	IMPALED	FESTIVITY	SHAMBLING
PERILOUS	MIMICKED	CONFOUNDING	PENETRATE	CULPRIT

Slave Dancer Vocabulary

INGENIOUS	MORTIFIED	DEBASED	PERPLEXED	ATHWART
CHANDLER	FLOGGED	WHEEDLING	PROTESTATIONS	ASSUAGE
MARTIAL	PLACIDLY	FREE SPACE	HARROWING	FETID
APOTHECARY	LUMINOUS	RESTRAINT	CAPTIOUS	UNCHARITABLE
DEMENTED	HOLYSTONED	AFFLICTION	TURBULENT	CONVULSION

Slave Dancer Vocabulary

PRESSGANGED	CABOCIERO	SPRY	BRINY	TRANQUIL
REFLECTIVELY	MIMICKED	CLAMOR	CAPTIOUS	CHAGRINED
CULPRIT	LOFTY	FREE SPACE	CONVULSION	PLACIDLY
ASSUAGE	IMPASSIVELY	MUTINIES	DEMENTED	SUSTAINED
ADDLES	BEGRIMED	MARTIAL	UNCHARITABLE	PENETRATE

Slave Dancer Vocabulary

WRACK	FLOGGED	REVIVIFIED	CHANDLER	ALOOFNESS
LUDICROUS	RECUMBENT	CONFOUNDING	AMIABLY	IMPERTINENT
WHEEDLING	DEFIED	FREE SPACE	CHAOS	APOTHECARY
MELANCHOLY	PROTESTATIONS	PROFUSION	AFFLICTION	INDISTINCT
LANGUOROUS	FETID	UNDETERRED	KEENING	PLIGHT

www.ingramcontent.com/pod-product-compliance
Lightning Source LLC
Chambersburg PA
CBHW081453070526
44586CB00019B/2332